# Swifter
## than the arrow

### Wilfred Bartrop, football and war

# Swifter
## than the arrow

### Wilfred Bartrop, football and war

*[signature]*

## Peter Holland

Matador
9 De Montfort Mews
Leicester LE1 7FW, UK
Tel: (+44) 116 255 9311 / 9312
Email: books@troubador.co.uk
Web: www.troubador.co.uk/matador

Picture credits: Front cover photo by Randall of Barnsley; Garside's Yard, photograph courtesy of
Nottinghamshire Local Studies and www.picturethepast.org.uk; Priorwell Road, photograph by Ezra
Taylor; Bennie Bartrop, courtesy of June Guirdham; Barnsley vs. QPR cartoon, Barnsley Independent;
Dubonnet Cup match, Borough Press, Swindon; open-top bus, originally from Mr. J. Jennings and Mrs. E.
Marfleet reproduced with permission of Barnsley Chronicle; medal, photographs courtesy of Bonhams;
Ruby Millership, courtesy of Mike Mitchell; marriage certificate is Crown copyright reproduced with
permission Controller of HMSO and Queen's Printer for Scotland; Wilfred Bartrop, courtesy of June
Guirdham; Manton Colliery, photograph by Ezra Taylor; yellow cross gas, photograph by the author used
with permission of the Memorial Museum Passchendaele; Freddie Wheatcroft, photograph by Protheroe &
Simons; Anneux cemetery, photograph by the author; Trench Mortar, stereoview photograph by
Underwood; the remains of Cambrai, reproduced from Photos of the Great War www.gwpda.org originally
sourced from Library of Congress; Canal du Nord, River Escaut, Warcoing cemetery, photographs by the
author; original source of other photographs could not be traced.

ISBN 978 1848760 684

Cataloguing-in-Publication (CIP) catalogue record
for this book is available from the British Library.

Typeset in 11pt Bembo by Troubador Publishing Ltd, Leicester, UK
Printed in the UK by TJ International, Padstow, Cornwall

**Matador** is an imprint of Troubador Publishing Ltd

To the memory of Arnold and Mary Jane Bartrop

# Contents

# Foreword

Like Wilfred Bartrop, I too was born in Worksop, although my family moved to Scunthorpe when I was only two years old. Nonetheless, I remember the many visits we made during my childhood to my maternal grandparents who lived in Hardwick Crescent, very close to Manton Colliery. This is where my grandfather William (Bill) Marsh worked, around the same time as Wilfred Bartrop, and was followed there later by my uncles Tom, Frank and Ken.

Bill Shankly, the successful and charismatic Liverpool FC manager has for many years been erroneously quoted as saying that 'Football is more important than life or death'. This book puts that all into perspective, as Bill himself would have done. 'Swifter than the Arrow' recounts the fascinating true story of a Worksop lad's professional football career, in which he enjoys phenomenal success with Barnsley and is transferred to the mighty Liverpool, before the First World War brings his career to an end.

After reading this book, I am proud to say that I was born in the same town as Wilfred, a man who was skillful enough to have a successful career in professional football, but also knew where his duty lay when called upon.

Graham Taylor OBE
Former Manager of Lincoln City FC, Watford FC, Aston Villa FC,
Wolverhampton Wanderers FC and the England National Football Team

# Acknowledgements

Many people have helped during the writing of this book, by providing a wealth of memories, photographs, press cuttings and advice. Arnold Bartrop was the first to mention Wilfred to me many years ago, but it was Arthur Bower and David Wood of Barnsley Football Club, and Peter Holme of the National Football Museum, who really got me started on the Wilf trail. Special thanks are due to Arthur Bower for his continued interest and for sharing his knowledge of the history of Barnsley Football Club, and to Rosalie Bower for her hospitality. Jonny Stokkeland and Eric Doig also deserve special mention for their detective work into the history of Liverpool Football Club. Other football teams came into the story, notably Manchester United, Worksop Town and Swindon Town, and I am indebted to the work of the club historians and supporters who have tirelessly recorded information. The same is true for historians of the Great War, and of these I particularly thank Andrew Jackson, Chris Baker, Kevin Dowson, Maggie Tyler and John Wainwright for clues and information. Another historian, Michael J. Jackson, was also a great help to my research into Victorian and Edwardian Worksop. David Wood, Arthur Bower, Daniel Parker, David Greaves, Michael J. Jackson, Paul Plowman, Mike Mitchell, June Guirdham, Pierre Vandervelden and an anonymous collector kindly allowed me to use photographs, as did Robert Cockroft of the *Barnsley Chronicle*, Arnie of lfchistory.net, Dan Davies and Chris Hayes of Bonhams, and Franky Bostyn of the Memorial Museum Passchendaele. Nick Tomlinson provided the photograph of Garside's yard from the excellent Nottinghamshire Local Studies and www.picturethepast.org.uk collection, while the Scottish Screen

Archive provided a short film of the 1912 Cup Final. In a few cases I was unable to trace the original source of a photograph, and I apologize if I have omitted to acknowledge the source in these cases. June Guirdham, Bob Guirdham, Dawn Storer, William Bartrop, Anne Fisher, Lindy Shipman, Doug Stanley, Joan Stanley, Mike Mitchell, Nicola Simpson and Frances Hall, all relatives of Wilfred or Ruby, were extremely generous with their time and it was a delight to talk to them. Tracing Wilfred's family and his life would not have been possible without access to the England and Wales Birth, Marriage and Death Index, the Census Records, the British Library Newspapers collection, the archives at Worksop, Nottingham and Liverpool libraries, and the remarkable resources at the National Archives in Kew. Wilfred and Ruby's marriage certificate is Crown Copyright and reproduced under licence from the Controller of HMSO and Queen's Printer for Scotland. I am indebted to Philip Waller for providing insightful comments on the entire text and for discussions on the historical context. I also thank Graham Taylor and Michael Parkinson for reading the text and for their encouragement, and Terry Compton, Jeremy Thompson, Amy Cooke and Julia Fuller at Troubador for their advice and professionalism. Finally, particular thanks go to Amanda, Pip and Jody for getting involved in the Wilf saga so enthusiastically, despite being dragged from Worksop to Warcoing, and from Barnsley to Bourlon Wood. It was an experience for us all.

Chapter 1

# The Bartrops of Worksop

A t first it is hard to recognize. The smooth, dome-shaped object is just a few inches across, grey and clearly very old. A fragment of bone perhaps? Something sharp protrudes from one side. The dim lighting in the huge church makes it hard to see precisely. Looking closer, it is the remains of a human skull, many centuries old, and with the shaft of an arrow embedded in the aged bone. According to local legend, the unlucky victim was a woodman killed 800 years ago in nearby Sherwood Forest. And the bow that fired the deadly arrow? Reputedly in the hands of the most famous archer of all time: Robin Hood. Today the skull and arrow rest in a small glass-covered alcove inside the impressive Priory Church that has stood in the town of Worksop in Nottinghamshire since the twelfth century.

Worksop has a long history. In the Domesday Book, compiled over 900 years ago, shortly after the Norman Conquest, Worksop or Werchesope was already an established agricultural community, with its various land owners ready and waiting to be taxed:

> In Werchesope (Worksop) Alfsi had three carucates of land taxable. Land for eight ploughs. Roger has one plough in lordship and twenty-two freemen with twelve bovates of this land and twenty-four villagers and eight smallholders who have twenty-two ploughs. Meadow, seven acres; woodland pasture two leagues long and three furlongs wide. Value before 1066 £8; now £7.[1]

Worksop was valued at seven pounds. William the Conqueror distributed the lands, and in time the region around Worksop came into the hands of Baron William de Lovetot. This was fortuitous in the long-term, because Lovetot was a benevolent man who gave lands to the poor, built a hospital for the sick and, in his most lasting legacy, founded the enormous Augustinian Priory that still towers over the town today. If Robin Hood and his men really existed, and there are plenty of indications that they did, they must have known this place well. Worksop at the time was a very small community, where everyone will have known everyone, so the comings and goings of fugitives from the forest would not go unnoticed. Indeed, the nearby town of Warsop may even derive its name from the Old English 'Waerg hop' meaning 'valley of the outlaws'.

Unlike some of its neighbours, Worksop remained a small town for most of its history, and even by 1801 its population was barely three thousand. This was to change rapidly. Just a hundred years later, the population had grown to sixteen thousand as the town experienced its first major boom. It is not hard to see why. Lying between the cities of Sheffield and Nottingham, Worksop is 250 miles from the Scottish border and 270 miles from the south coast of England, and also midway between the east and west coasts. It is at the very centre of England. In the nineteenth century, canals and railways were changing the face of the country and as a consequence, accidents of geography often governed a town's prospects. The Chesterfield Canal was built through the town, as was the Manchester, Sheffield and Lincolnshire Railway, and Worksop now found itself at the fulcrum of communication and distribution routes. Furthermore, rich seams of coal were discovered close to town, and several productive mines were sunk to reach the 'black gold' needed to fuel the burgeoning industrial revolution.

Worksop in the late 1800s was a town where manufacturing, mining, commerce and distribution industries were all thriving. This may sound a picture of prosperity, but for most of the working men, women and children, things were not quite so rosy. Life was hard for the average worker in Victorian England, whether one worked on the canals, on the railways, down the mines, in the breweries or in the woodyards.

Although leisure time was limited, this was also a time when sport was beginning to emerge as a serious enterprise. There are records of cricket matches being played in Worksop in the early 1800s and by the middle of the century there was a thriving cricket club. Football came later, but a small club was founded around 1875 that played occasional matches on a field owned by a local corn miller. In 1887, the cricket and football clubs merged under the presidency of Mr William Allen and soon afterwards semi-professional football was being played in Worksop. This marked a major new direction — now sport was not just about participation, it also offered something for the spectator. Crowds of several hundred would gather to watch Worksop Town's early matches. One of the players they watched was a sporting hero whose name has now been largely forgotten. He was a footballer who played at the highest level of the English game and who competed against some of Europe's most famous teams. As a sportsman, he won medals, honours and trophies, before responding to his country's call when the world descended into war. His name was Wilfred Bartrop.

Wilfred Bartrop was born in 1889 and joined his local football club Worksop Town at the age of 18. A year later he was signed by Barnsley Football Club where he enjoyed phenomenal success for five seasons before a transfer to First Division side Liverpool FC. At least that is the history according to the Football League. The truth is that no Wilfred Bartrop was born in 1889 — not in Worksop, or indeed anywhere. In fact, Charles Henry Wilfred Bartrop, to give him his full name, was born in Worksop two years earlier, on 22 November 1887. We will never know if a genuine mistake was made concerning his age, or whether Wilfred was being somewhat economical with the truth, but once his 'new age' had been set it stayed with him for the rest of his life. Perhaps he simply thought that he had more chance of being signed as a professional footballer if his club thought he was 18 or 19, rather than almost 22 years old? Despite Alan Hansen's famous jibe that 'you'll never win anything with kids',[2] it is obvious that a player signed at 19 years old should have a long playing career in front of him. Whatever the reason, Wilfred was actually almost 22 when he signed for Barnsley FC, and an experienced player of 26 when he joined Liverpool FC.

Charles Henry Wilfred Bartrop never used his first name during his football career or later when he enlisted in the army. He simply preferred the name Wilfred. We also know that his parents called him by the name Wilfred when he was young, as this is how he is recorded in the 1891 national census that took place when he was three years old. In the 1901 census, when he was a teenager, he is recorded Chas Hy W, but it seems that on this occasion the official census recorder for Worksop was being particularly fussy, because each member of his family has all their initials recorded!

Bartrop is a rare surname in most of England, but is relatively common around the Worksop area of Nottinghamshire and in the West Riding of Yorkshire. There are numerous variants of the surname in existence today because, as with all surnames, changes in spelling were commonplace before official registration of births, marriages and deaths began in 1837, when most people were illiterate. Wilfred Bartrop was descended from John Barthorpe, born in 1797 in the hamlet of Elksley, near Worksop, and his wife Hannah, born in 1793 in the village of Ranby. John and Hannah moved into the growing town of Worksop, where John took work as a boatman on the Chesterfield Canal. In the 1840s, John and Hannah's eldest son, Benjamin, joined his father on the canal which ran close to their homes on Church Walk, starting on a wage of eightpence per day.[3] Benjamin, who now used the surname Bartrop rather than Barthorpe, worked as a boatman for the next twenty-five years.

The Chesterfield Canal was officially opened in 1777, and played an important role in the development of towns and villages in Nottinghamshire. The canal affected everybody living in and around Worksop. One immediate benefit was that the price of coal almost halved, dropping from 7d or 8d a hundredweight to 4½d.[4] The canal was originally 46 miles long, running from Chesterfield in the Peak District to the River Trent at Stockwith, and was built to carry iron ore mined from the Peak District and coal from Nottinghamshire. The cargo would be taken in narrow horse-drawn barges along the canal before being loaded onto boats on the River Trent and carried out into the North Sea for distribution to other ports. Stone extracted from the many local quarries followed the same route, and was an important resource for some major building works around the country. Perhaps the most famous of these was the rebuilding of the Houses of Parliament in London. The original Palace of Westminster and the Parliament building were destroyed by a fire in 1834, and rebuilding work took place over the next thirty years. The new Houses of Parliament were to include the impressive 320ft clock tower housing the giant bell, Big Ben, and the largest clock face in Britain. Wilfred Bartrop's grandfather Benjamin, and great-grandfather John, both worked on the Chesterfield Canal at a time when vast quantities of Nottinghamshire stone were taken along it, through Worksop, on their way to build one of England's most impressive landmarks.

The principal cargo that Benjamin Bartrop transported most days was not stone, but coal. His employer was Joseph Garside, a rich and successful businessman who ran a large timber yard in Worksop, employing over a hundred men, and also owned the Priorwell brewery. Both were sited next to the canal. Benjamin first joined the employment of the Garside family when he was still a teenager, working on the canal boats that brought the coal to fuel the timber yard boiler. Over the next decade, he rose to become Garside's master boatman, a senior and responsible job.[5] The work was hard, however, involving strenuous loading and unloading of coal in all weathers, usually by hand with just a shovel. Furthermore, the Chesterfield Canal had several tunnels where there was no tow-path for horses, and here manpower had to take over. The boatman would lie on his back, on top of the cargo, and 'leg' the heavily laden, twenty-yard boat through the tunnel, often with just a few inches between his face and the dark tunnel roof. With the massive Norwood tunnel just west of Worksop stretching for over a mile and a half, this would have been back-breaking work.

Benjamin Bartrop married Jane Coupe on 23 June 1856. Over the next 15 years they had 10 children, before Jane died of typhoid fever aged just 33. Infectious diseases were then commonplace in the area, as standards of sanitation were very poor. Benjamin and Jane lived on Church Walk, a small street in Worksop still present today. Next door lived Benjamin's parents John and Hannah. Contemporary accounts paint a grim picture of life in their neighbourhood.

In a yard in Church Walk was a row of five houses, 'in every one of which' Mr Hase said 'there has been fever'. There was an inaccessible drain, or ditch, between two rows of houses, 'where no current of air could penetrate. The premises contain, in addition, three or four privies, about five manure heaps, and eight piggeries'. ... In the same neighbourhood were the gasworks, and Mr John Hancock complained of the stench therefrom, combined with the odour arising from a drain near his premises. Two of his men had died within three months, and he thought they were injured by the stench.[6]

There was no proper water supply and no sewer, with the privies empting into open ditches between the houses. A local doctor, John Trethick, who was one of many campaigning for improved sanitation in Worksop, alleged that the gutters of the main streets 'ran with liquid manure'.[7]

Workers from Joseph Garside's Timber Yard, around 1900. Wilfred's grandfather, aged about 70, was still employed as a drayman and could be leading the horses

Soon after Jane's death, and now in his forties, Benjamin stopped working on the canal. He did not, however, leave the employment of the influential Joseph Garside. Around 1880, together with his second wife Mary Broom, Benjamin moved away from Church Walk to live in one of the cottages bordering Garside's timber yard, where he now worked as a labourer, and later as a drayman, handling the shire horses used in the business. In many ways it was a natural development from his days as a boatman, because all the working boats on the Chesterfield Canal were horse-drawn. His new job simply continued his work with heavy horses. As a drayman he would drive the open-sided wagons or 'drays' to deliver wood from the timber yard, and beer from the brewery, around the county of Nottinghamshire. These journeys were slow and could take several days. For example, on 3 April 1881 Benjamin is recorded as staying overnight at the Pauncefote Arms in East Stoke, not far outside Worksop. He had spent at least two days delivering Garside's Priorwell Ale to an inn a mere 30 miles away – and presumably being conscientious enough to stay a while to check the quality of a few pints.

Benjamin Bartrop was one of longest serving employees of the Garside family, providing 52 years service, and when Joseph Garside died in 1893 Benjamin was one of his coffin bearers.[8] A contemporary described 'Drugger' Bartrop as 'a fine specimen of the steady, industrious and painstaking artisan, a man who enjoyed the confidence of his employer, and the respect of his neighbours'.[9] Several of Benjamin's children also found work in Garside's timber yard, including his son William from his second marriage, and another son (also called Benjamin or more usually Bennie) from his first marriage; both of the young men worked with horses. Bennie was to become Wilfred Bartrop's father.

Bennie Bartrop was born in Worksop in 1860. As a young man, he had seen an attractive teenage girl, Annie Maria, walking around the town, and had told her 'One day, you'll be my wife'.[10] His confidence was well placed. When he was aged 27, Bennie married 19-year old Annie Maria Jarvis at the Parish Church, Worksop, and the couple moved into 13 Priorwell Road, bordering Garside's timber yard and close to the Priory Church. Their first child, Charles Henry Wilfred, was born eight weeks later. Wilfred was born at Annie Maria's parents' house, just next door at 11 Priorwell Road. Although the street still exists, the house in which Wilfred the footballer was born is not standing. In 1894, the Duke of Newcastle funded improvements to several roads in Worksop, including Priorwell Road and the Priory Gate House. Numbers 11 and 13 were probably replaced during this redevelopment. By 1901, when Wilfred was a young teenager, the family moved to Canal Terrace, a row of tiny cottages across the road from Garside's brewery, where Bennie now worked. The cottages are still standing, and provide an evocative picture of workers' homes of the 1890s. But even this was not to prove permanent, and soon the family moved further south to Pelham Street, and then to a terraced house in Clinton Street on the eastern edge of Worksop, bordered by allotments and fields.

A view down Priorwell Road from the canal bridge in the early part of the twentieth century. The road on the left led to Joseph Garside's timber yard, while opposite was the gate to his brewery. The Priory Church is visible in the distance.
Wilfred Bartrop was born in a house on this road

Wilfred was part of a large family. His father had nine brothers and sisters (although several died as infants), plus several half-brothers and sisters, almost all of whom lived in Worksop. When growing up, young Wilfred had uncles, aunts and cousins on almost every street in the neighbourhood. His parents also played their own part in expanding the Bartrop population of Worksop, because Wilfred himself was the first of thirteen children. His brothers and sisters were each given names almost as elaborate as his own, despite the fact that middle names were quite unusual at the time. After Charles Henry Wilfred, the younger children in the family were Percy Frederick, Ethel Marion, Elsie May, Violet Evelyn, Arthur Ernest, Walter Alfred, Cecil William, Bertie Reginald, Ivy, Cyril Bernard, Mabel Lilian and Bernard William.

Wilfred's father, Bennie Bartrop, spent most of his life working with horses. He handled the horses for the Garside business, working at the timber yard and the brewery, and he was called upon to make deliveries just as his own father had done. Even as a young man, he would sometimes accompany Mr Garside in his horse and trap around the town, and on one occasion, when Bennie was still a teenager, the two were even thrown from the vehicle together. The local newspaper carried the story in alarmist style, reporting that 'On Monday afternoon, about 5 o'clock an accident occurred to Mr Joseph Garside … Mr Garside and the youth who was with him, named Bartrop, were pitched head foremost over the front of the trap and over the horse. Mr Garside fell heavily on his head under the arch of the (Priory) Gatehouse and his forehead was much cut and bruised. The boy fell partly under his master, and sustained injuries to his leg'.[11] The newspaper reported in detail the medical treatment given to Garside, and reassured readers that he was well on the road to recovery. No mention was made of how the young Bartrop was faring.

Much later in life Bennie Bartrop was promoted to became Joseph Garside's groom,[12] an important job that could be entrusted only to one of his most reliable employees. Every Sunday, Bennie was called upon to drive Mr Garside and other members of 'the gentry', as he always called them,[13] to the Priory Church by horse and carriage. Many years later, well into his eighties, Bennie – with a shock of white hair and carefully groomed white moustache – would sit in his chair, recounting the old days or singing the well-known 1930s radio advertisement:[14]

We are the Ovaltineys, little girls and boys;
Make your requests, we'll not refuse you;
We are here just to amuse you;
Would you like a song or story?
Will you share our joys?
At games and sports we're more than keen;
No merrier children could be seen;
Because we all drink Ovaltine;
We're happy girls and boys.[15]

Benjamin (Bennie) Bartrop

Bennie's pipe, fitted with a sauce bottle-top with holes knocked through to stop the sparks, would be ever present.[16] And much of the talk, of course, was about horses.

It must have been a natural expectation that Bennie's eldest son, Wilfred, would follow in his father's and grandfather's footsteps. His stocky, muscular build was ideal for handling horses, and for the manual work around the timber yard and brewery. However, in 1902 another major industry had started in the Worksop area with the sinking of Manton Colliery. Hundreds of young men gained work at the colliery, and several of Wilfred's own brothers spent many years as coal miners at Manton. For Wilfred, however, such work did not last for long. Wilfred had another skill, and other plans.

## Chapter 2

## Shamrocks and Pensioners

I n 1908, at the age of 20, Wilfred Bartrop joined his local football
club, Worksop Town FC, then playing in the Midland League.
Worksop Town were not excelling at that point in their history. In
the 1906/07 season they had finished fourteenth out of twenty clubs
and their league form in 1907/08 was not much better. But in January
1908, football fever was gripping the town. After narrowly beating
Castleford Town in the fourth qualifying round of the FA Cup,
Worksop Town had drawn the mighty Chelsea FC in the first round
proper. The eagerly awaited match was originally to be played in
Worksop, but the teams agreed to switch it to Stamford Bridge in
London so as to benefit from larger gate receipts. The Pensioners, as
Chelsea were known then, were not the billionaire-backed force they
are today, but they were still a well-positioned team in Division One
and many leagues above Worksop Town. They were also an entirely
professional team able to pay their players full-time wages, whereas
Worksop Town's players had other jobs. The words of one reporter,
written in 1908, still have a surprising familiarity about them today,
when he described the 'great' Chelsea as 'a club which has simply
forced its way to the front by means of illimitable wealth'.[1]

Wilfred Bartrop did not play for Worksop Town in that match, but he
may have been one of 18,995 who witnessed a 9–1 demolition inflicted
by the First Division team.[2] Remarkably, this still stands as Chelsea's
largest ever domestic victory, a century later. The game also still holds
the Chelsea record for the most goals scored by one player. Chelsea
centre forward George 'Gatling Gun' Hilsdon, who in 1906 had scored

five in his debut game against Glossop, went one better by scoring six of the goals against Worksop Town (if it is any consolation, a partisan reporter thought the sixth was scored from a 'decidedly off side position').[3] The game itself was played in almost a party atmosphere, with brass bands before kick off and the large Chelsea crowd cheering the play of both teams. There were also several moments of hilarity for the crowd, caused by the slippery nature of the pitch. The ground was just thawing after an icy spell, and although the Chelsea players sensibly wore studded boots to grip in the wet ground, the Worksop Town team did not possess such new fangled equipment, causing all sorts of problems. The crowd roared with laughter every time one of the battling Worksop players slipped or slithered, although it was no laughing matter for the players. Not only did it in leave Worksop Town at a distinct disadvantage when the ball was in play, but two of their players were injured by falls and in the second half they only ever had ten men on the field at any one time.

After the match, or rather the mismatch, the teams dined together at the Gaiety Restaurant on the Strand. Reports reveal a very grand dinner with a football theme throughout, accompanied by indoor fireworks and finishing with a giant iced pudding surmounted by a footballer carved out of a solid block of ice. The occasion was especially convivial, held in the spirit of celebrating the first match between two teams far apart both geographically and in sporting achievement. The Gaiety Restaurant had even erected goalposts at each side of the dining table, and hung these with ten illuminated footballs, corresponding to the number of goals scored. It was just an unfortunate oversight of the proprietors that the balls were 'of the rugger shape instead of the soccer'.[4]

During the winter of the 1907/08 season, the 'Shamrocks' were having a torrid time. Worksop Town had earned their nickname on account of their green strip, just as today's Worksop players, in yellow and black, are known as the 'Tigers'. The weekly football correspondent for the *Worksop Guardian*, a pithy and critical observer who wrote under the pseudonym 'Wide-Awake' was not impressed with their run of form. Under the heading 'A Terrible Weekend' he announced 'It is my doleful duty to record the tidings of the terrible experiences undergone by the Worksop Town team last week-end'.[5] Heavy defeats inflicted by Nottingham Forest Reserves and Lincoln had sent Wide-Awake into despair. The team management also agreed that something was wrong, and in came two new players from the reserves: Watkinson in midfield (half-back) and Bartrop as an inside-forward or striker. The next game to be played was on 7 March 1908, at home against arch rivals Rotherham Town.

Bartrop's debut was a disaster. Not only did Worksop Town lose 2–1, causing discontented murmurings from the crowd, but it was clear where much of the fault lay. The two new players were just not up to the task. Wide-Awake tried not to blame the debutants directly saying they were both 'promising players', but he certainly felt the management had got it wrong by bringing them in for such an important game. 'The committee probably realise, now it is too late, the mistake of playing men in a class much above them'.[6] And in a sniping opening paragraph, he wrote: 'It may be that some of the Worksop players have been out of form lately, but to supersede them for a match of this importance, in favour of men whose experience has been limited to football of a very elementary class, was to say the least, no great mark of superlative wisdom'.[7] Not that the committee's selection of the debutants was solely responsible for the defeat and – with the protection of his pseudonym – Wide-Awake roundly declared that one of the regular players, Parramore, gave 'his weakest display of the season' while another, Cooke, was 'almost useless'.[8]

Wilfred Bartrop was promptly dropped for the following game, away to Newark. It made little difference as Worksop Town were thrashed 4–1. On the same day, however, Bartrop scored twice for the reserves, earning a 2–2 draw with the Atlas and Norfolk Works team, in a performance that managed to extract a morsel of praise from the ever-critical Wide-Awake. 'Bartrop played a good game, and with experience should develop into a useful man'.[9] Before long, Bartrop had fought his way back into the first team and for the last couple of months of the 1907/08 season he was a regular selection for the Shamrocks, finishing the season with ten first team games under his belt and one goal. One of the most significant events in this period occurred on 28 March 1908, in a win against Bradford City Reserves. For this game an experimental attacking line was tried with Bartrop on the right wing for the first time, instead of in the centre of the attack. It was a sensible move that made use of his pace, dribbling skills and crossing abilities (and, to be honest, lack of a finishing instinct); and it made all the difference to his game. He stayed in this position until the end of his career.

Over the Easter weekend of 1908, Worksop Town played three matches – on Good Friday, Saturday and Easter Monday – with the players getting only Easter Sunday as a break. Worksop Town played with great determination in each game and were very unlucky to finish the holiday period with one win and two defeats. On Good Friday afternoon, the weather was unseasonably sunny and the day had 'everything in favour of outdoor enjoyment'.[10] A crowd of over two thousand turned out to watch the visit of Chesterfield Reserves. Despite Worksop going behind in the first five minutes, the home supporters were rewarded in the end as Worksop Town eventually sneaked home 2–1 winners. Bartrop was instrumental in the second goal, whipping a corner into the box to be met by the head of George Padley. The third Easter game, an away match to Barnsley Reserves was more disappointing, with Worksop losing 2–1. However, at least the result could be put down to bad luck rather than poor play. Worksop had an early goal disallowed unfairly, before going a goal down, equalising, then losing to a goal in the 87th minute following a mix-up between Bartrop and Armitage, who each let the ball run past. It was particularly unfortunate for Bartrop, as it had been his work that had brought Worksop Town back into the game, when his fierce cross was deflected into the Barnsley goal off a defender for the equaliser.

But it was the game held on Easter Saturday, after the Chesterfield win and before the Barnsley defeat, which generated most headlines. Worksop Town were the visitors to Doncaster Rovers, a team propping up the bottom of the Midland League in the 1907/08 season. This was also a team with a reputation for particularly rowdy supporters, and as a result the club authorities had already been called to answer to the

Football Association earlier in the season. The match was a hard fought affair, with chances falling to both sides and Worksop having a good shot cleared off the line. With the game reaching the 88th minute, and the score still at 0–0, Doncaster Rovers eventually succeeded in forcing the ball into the Worksop net. However, the forward had been fouled in the build up to the goal, and bizarrely the referee decided to call play back and award a penalty kick to Doncaster. Tensions were now running high. Despite the pressure, Ben Jones, the popular Doncaster Rovers forward, calmly converted the penalty to the delight of the boisterous home support. Almost from the restart, the ball broke to Jones again and he raced towards the Worksop goal accompanied by a frenzied roar. Just in time, Worksop Town defender E. W. Gregory dived in and brought Jones crashing to the ground with a heavy challenge.

Accounts of the incident differ depending on whether one believes newspaper reports from Doncaster or from Worksop. The striker was either brought down by 'a running kick… catching him in a most dangerous place'[11] or 'not by any mean means unfairly'.[12] Jones had to be carried from the field of play and when the referee's final whistle sounded just seconds later, the ground erupted. Spectators surged onto the pitch, most of them surrounding the unfortunate Worksop Town youngster Watkinson who had been mistaken for his hard-tackling team mate! Watkinson was pushed to the ground and kicked by angry supporters, and it took the brave intervention of the Worksop goalkeeper to rescue him, despite receiving several blows to the head himself. One of the linesmen was also attacked before the Worksop team was finally escorted safely to the dressing room, to nurse their wounds and their defeat. Not surprisingly, for Doncaster Rovers it meant a second summons to meet the officials at the Football Association.

The season ended two games later, with Worksop Town finishing in a respectable eighth position out of twenty teams in the Midland league. Sheffield Wednesday Reserves were deserved champions, and underlined their class with an 8–1 demolition of Worksop Town on the last day of the season. But Worksop could take some positives from the season, or at least the latter part of it. Their home record was exceptional with fourteen wins, five draws and just a single defeat. Their away record was best forgotten. They had battled through the qualifying rounds to reach the first round proper of the FA Cup, and had enjoyed the memorable game away to Chelsea. Club finances were in a good state, helped partly by the visit to Stamford Bridge, and also by the transfer of right back Coupe to Manchester City for £150. An agreement had also been secured with the Worksop Cricket Club for the football club to continue using the 'Town Ground' for another five years. And, perhaps most importantly, considerable promise was being shown by the young players who were brought in half way through the season. Four of these, Bartrop, Watkinson, Wright and Lemmons, were all promptly signed for the following season.

Towards the end of summer, the football club started its preparations for the 1908/09 campaign. This was also to be Wilfred Bartrop's first full season with Worksop Town.

A series of practice matches and trials were held behind the cricket pavilion, and watched by crowds all eagerly looking forward to the new season. Optimism was high. Within a week of the start, however, players and supporters suffered a sharp reality check. The mood was summed up by Wide-Awake in his usual lyrical style:

> Football is with us again, bringing its joys and its disappointments, its foregone conclusions and its surprises, and already a good many castles built in the air during the close season have evaporated before the logic of hard facts. It is ever thus; no team in the country opens the season without announcing to the world that its prospects are brighter than at any period of its existence, and hopes are raised that must inevitably be shattered in the first few weeks of September.[13]

Worksop Town began the season with an away defeat to Barnsley Reserves, and followed that with what, in many ways, was an even more disappointing result. In a home match against Notts County Reserves, Worksop stormed ahead to a 4–1 lead at half-time, including a penalty won and converted by Wilfred Bartrop. In the second half, however, the Worksop players ran out of energy and ideas, letting in three soft goals and capitulating to a tame draw. Fitness levels, communication and determination were all to be questioned. Wide-Awake commented that 'In the first half Bartrop showed dazzling form, but afterwards he faded away to nothing'.[14] The same could have been said of the whole team.

It was not simply a poor start to the season: it was a taste of things to come. After seven games, the record was a sorry one of four defeats, one draw and only two wins: just five points from a possible fourteen. Four months and many more defeats later, Worksop Town were rooted to the bottom of the Midland League. Maintaining their status in the Midland League now looked under pressure. By the end of the 1908/09 season, it was only the even more dismal form of Leeds City Reserves that kept Worksop off bottom spot, but the Shamrocks could not be satisfied with their own tally of 21 games lost, 7 drawn and 10 won.

Wide-Awake for one was looking forward to reporting on the cricket season rather than football. 'The term has been a most depressing one for both players, officials and supporters, all of whom will say farewell to the winter game with few regrets'[15] he wrote. The only redeeming feature of the season was the form shown by the younger players, notably Wilfred Bartrop and Grayson Wright. It was a real coup for the club that these two were selected to represent the 'Rest of the Midlands' in a summer competition against the league champions. In just over a year, Bartrop had gone from being pilloried as substandard, to being recognised as one of the best players in the team and indeed in the whole league.

With the added exposure of representing the 'Rest of the Midlands', it came as no surprise that one of the fully professional teams would move to sign Bartrop. On 21 June 1909, the inevitable happened. Barnsley Football Club secured Bartrop's transfer for what was reported as 'a substantial sum'.[16]

# Chapter 3

# Battling Barnsley

Football has a long history, and the game as played today gradually emerged during the reign of Queen Victoria. In 1848, representatives of five English public schools met in Trinity College, Cambridge, and agreed on a set of rules for the game of football. The 'Cambridge Rules' were influential in the academic arena, but they were not universally accepted by other clubs. What was needed was a set of guidelines and laws to be followed by everyone. On 26 October 1863, eleven leading clubs met in London and founded an all-encompassing governing body for the game: the Football Association. The FA set about amending and standardising the laws of the game, but football still retained many elements that seem unfamiliar today. For example, in 1863 ends were changed after each goal, and catching the ball was an active part of the game. Corner kicks were not introduced until 1872, the same year that the FA Cup was first held. The English Football League commenced much later, with the 1888/89 season. Professionalism was forbidden in the early years and only became accepted and legalised in 1885, although not until after Preston North End had been expelled from the FA Cup in 1884 for paying their players.

By the start of the twentieth century, when Wilfred Bartrop played, the organisation of the game in England had many more resemblances to football today. The football league comprised two Divisions each containing 20 professional teams, with relegation and promotion between Divisions One and Two. Players were being transferred between the top teams for substantial sums, and in 1905 the first £1000 transfer took place: Alf Common moving from Sunderland to Middlesbrough. Not that the concept of transfers was universally approved of. Many observers of the game felt that the movement of players around the country was removing the local nature of each team, while the buying and selling of people was reminiscent of darker days. A correspondent to *The Times* in 1911 summed up a common view when he commented that transfers were 'a disgrace to the game and blot on British sportsmanship'.[1]

There was still a maximum wage payable to footballers, but players were showing some disgruntlement over their level of pay. In 1908 Billy Meredith of Manchester United successfully spearheaded a campaign to increase the maximum wage from £4 to £5 per week, thereby striking the first victory for player power. This was an exceptionally good wage for the time, more than twice the sum earned by even skilled workers. In the early years of the twentieth century there was much debate about the legality of the maximum wage system and a general feeling that it could not last long. In fact, at an Extraordinary General Meeting of the FA held on 22 April 1910, the decision was made to delete all reference to a maximum wage from the official rules, leaving the matter to the clubs. Nonetheless, the system essentially stayed in place, though less rigorously adhered to. This remained the case right up to 1961, when negotiations led by Jimmy Hill, on behalf of the Professional Footballers' Association, finally saw the system being scrapped, by which time the agreed maximum wage had risen to just £20.

The top clubs attracted massive crowds, sometimes in excess of fifty thousand per game, and when the usual charge at the turnstiles was sixpence this meant that the big clubs had substantial incomes. Like the Premiership of today, there was already some stability in the top flight of English football, partly because of such clubs' large attendance figures and hefty gate receipts. Between 1900 and 1908, the most successful clubs were Manchester United, Liverpool, Sheffield Wednesday and Newcastle United. Of these, Newcastle United was the dominant force, winning the championship three times, and rarely dropping out of the top four.

Barnsley Football Club, founded in 1887 in connection with St Peter's Church, was not part of the elite group. Since entering the English league in 1898, the club had never risen out of the Second Division; the best finish being seventh place in the 1904/05 season. Barnsley FC finished the 1908/09 season in seventeenth place in Division Two, at the time their worst ever conclusion and one place lower than the previous season. The club finances were also in trouble and the manager Arthur Fairclough was forced to make changes. Fairclough sold one of his regular goalkeepers, and signed Fred Mearns from Hartlepool United as back-up for Jack Cooper. Although Hartlepool was a non-league club, Mearns did have First Division experience with Sunderland and with Bury. Two forwards were also signed in June: a scrawny but fast centre forward named Harry Tufnell and a pacy outside right with 'the build of a ploughman', Wilfred Bartrop.[2]

Tufnell, born in Burton-upon-Trent, was a real catch as he was already proving his worth to First Division club Bury. He was to go on to make 200 appearances for Barnsley, scoring 60 goals, including (as we will see later) the most famous goal in the club's history. In contrast to Mearns and Tufnell, Bartrop was not an established professional and Arthur Fairclough was taking a gamble on the muscular forward. He was not disappointed, however, and 'Barty' went on to make 160 appearances for Barnsley FC.

Wilfred Bartrop made his debut for Barnsley on 4 September 1909 in the second game of the 1909/10 season, playing against Glossop North End away. Barnsley lost 3–0, but despite the setback the reshaped team soon found its form. Before Christmas 1909, Barnsley had notched up a 5–1 victory over Birmingham City, a 7–0 demolition of Leeds City and a 7–1 win over Wolves, with Bartrop scoring his first goal for the club. But it was not in the league that Barnsley Football Club was to generate most excitement and publicity. Every year presents a golden opportunity for the lower-ranked clubs to pit themselves against the big guns: the FA Cup or 'English Cup' as it was originally called. People often speak of the romance of the FA Cup and for good reason. Not only is it the oldest football competition in the world, dating back to 1872, but it operates in such a way that it can spring a surprise at any stage. There are no league-type 'group stages' to even out form, no two-legged matches to give the bigger clubs an advantage, and no seeding to smooth the path for the glamour teams (apart from byes past the qualifying rounds). The simple knock-out system with a random draw at each round makes the FA Cup different from almost every other major competition, including the League Cup (started in 1960), the Champions League and even the World Cup. Every year the FA Cup throws up David versus Goliath pairings and the possibilities of giant killing. The FA Cup competition of 1910 was no different.

In 1910, the FA Cup first round saw 64 clubs in action: the 40 professional teams and 24 from the amateur leagues. Barnsley's opponents in the first round were Blackpool. On paper, this was a team in freefall: Blackpool had finished last in the First Division in 1909 and they were now heading for a bottom-half finish in the Second Division. The match was drawn 1–1, but in the replay on Election Day Barnsley stepped up a gear and won by an impressive six goals to nil. Another comprehensive win followed in the second round, with a 4–0 win over Bristol Rovers, in which Bartrop scored the first goal after 12 minutes. Bristol had in fact been drawn as the 'home' team for this round, but sold the choice of ground to Barnsley for £500; a decision they probably regretted after the match. The third round match against West Bromwich Albion was a much tighter affair, with centre forward Harry Tufnell scoring the only goal to put Barnsley through.

By the fourth round, excitement among the supporters had grown to an unprecedented level. This was not so much because of the opposition, Queen's Park Rangers, but because if this match was won Barnsley would be through to the semi-finals for the first time. On 5 March 1910, supporters headed into Barnsley from every town, village and hamlet in the vicinity. The attendance record for Oakwell was smashed, with 23,574 passing through the turnstiles and cramming onto the terraces.

So crowded were the spectators in some quarters that many persons were only able to catch glimpses of the game. All round the playing area was a surging sea of faces, and the spectacle was one to be long remembered… The waiting crowd, which was throughout good humoured notwithstanding some dangerous swaying movements found it very hot under the glaring sun, but they kept their positions firmly. Party colours were much in evidence, but the red and white of Barnsley greatly predominated.[3]

In the opening exchanges both teams had chances to score in a fast-paced end-to-end game. The breakthrough came midway through the first half. In the 25th minute, Tommy Boyle passed the ball out to Wilfred Bartrop on the right wing. Bartrop raced forward, and then almost as he reached the bye-line he unleashed a swerving ball towards goal. The ball flew past Tufnell and Lillycrop, who each tried in vain to get a head to it, beyond the leaping QPR goalkeeper, and against the upper part of the far post. It ricocheted into the back of the net. One experienced football reporter described it as 'bang on target… a beauty', and commented that 'it made players and onlookers alike open their eyes in wonder'.[4] Another ranked it as 'one of the greatest goals I ever saw'.[5] Some others who saw it were more surprised than impressed – surely Bartrop had meant it as a cross not a shot? As one curmudgeonly writer put it: 'Bartrop no more expected to score than I expect to win an English Cup medal'.[6]

Shot or cross, it mattered little. Barnsley had taken the lead. The man responsible was instantly mobbed by his team mates, with defender Dickie Downs going a step further in his celebrations than was normal in those formal, hand-shaking days. 'We were positive it was a cup-tie and not a comic opera, but Downs, Barnsley's full back dashed across to Bartrop after the goal had been scored, and gave the unlucky man a bare-faced kiss'.[7]

Remarkably, there still exists a photograph of Bartrop's goal, showing the leaping QPR goalkeeper just failing to reach the ball. Alas, there is no photograph of the goal celebration.

Wilfred Bartrop's winning goal in the fourth round of
the FA Cup, 5 March 1910

It was a classic cup-tie – exciting, vigorous and hard fought to the end.
And as is almost commonplace today (and always keenly anticipated),
as the final whistle approached the goalkeeper for the trailing team
rushed forward to join the attacking line. It was to no avail. Bartrop's
goal was to prove decisive. The Barnsley players could consider
themselves a little fortunate, but they were through to the last four.

Two First Division teams had also reached the semi-finals, Everton and
the favourites Newcastle United, the reigning league champions. As
with the cup today, each semi-final was to be played at a neutral venue.
Barnsley FC drew Everton with the match to be played in Leeds at
Elland Road, which probably suited the Yorkshire side as they had
memories of a 7–0 victory on that ground earlier in the season. The
supporters' excitement had now spread to the whole town of Barnsley,
and souvenirs were produced to celebrate the occasion. One postcard
shows a cartoon of Barnsley's mascot, Amos the donkey, stubbornly

Postcard celebrating Barnsley's win over QPR,
FA Cup fourth round, 1910

Cartoon celebrating Barnsley's win over QPR, depicting Bartrop's goal
FA Cup fourth round, 1910

refusing to budge on the road to Leeds. The caption read 'Amos, yer daft moke; we shan't get theer in time for th' kick off'.[8] The team plus thirty-five thousand supporters, and perhaps Amos the mascot, did get there in time – only to witness a disappointing goalless draw.

The replay took place five days later, on 31 March 1910, at Old Trafford in Manchester. This time fifty-five thousand supporters came through the gates, a massive crowd for a Thursday afternoon. Accounts of the match describe a highly entertaining game, and one with a fair degree of controversy. In the first half, both teams squandered chances to go ahead from the penalty spot, Barnsley's Tommy Boyle blasting wide and Everton's Jack Sharp seeing his kick superbly saved by Barnsley goalkeeper Fred Mearns. Those incidents don't tell the whole story, however, as Everton's performance was clearly affected by injuries to two of their players. Just fifteen minutes after the kick-off, Everton's Scottish international Jack Taylor received a severe kick to the neck, fracturing his larynx. The injury marked the end of his professional career, in which he had scored 66 goals for Everton in 400 appearances. Of more immediate concern, Everton were reduced to 10 men for the rest of the match (it would be more than half a century before substitutes were allowed). They were also forced to switch one of their forwards, Wattie White, back to a more defensive position, greatly lessening their goal threat.[9]

Just after the break, striker Ernie Gadsby put Barnsley in the lead, after a hectic scramble inside the Everton penalty area. The incident resulted in another injury to a key Everton player. In the struggle, goalkeeper Walter Scott suffered serious damage to his hand and had to leave the field for extensive treatment, thus forcing Everton to play on with just nine men. When he returned, his team was on the ropes. Incidentally, Wilfred Bartrop would have known Everton's goalkeeper well; both were born in Worksop, and both originally played for Worksop Town.

For most of the second half, Everton kept the Barnsley forwards at bay and the score at 1–0. Five minutes from full-time, however, Tom Forman scored a second goal for Barnsley, picking up a cross from Bartrop, and then just seconds after the re-start Harry Tufnell added a third. In the circumstances, Everton could consider themselves unlucky, but Barnsley's 3–0 victory had taken them through to the FA Cup Final. The half-time score had been telephoned back to the football club's headquarters in Barnsley, followed by further calls as the goals were scored, and in each case the news was passed instantly to the crowd of anxious supporters. The early editions of the newspapers were out soon after the final whistle, and the slightest information devoured by excited supporters.

As news of the victory spread, more and more people left their homes and gathered in the centre of Barnsley, or lining the approaches to the central rail station, in the hope of welcoming home their heroes. But it was not a footballer that the crowds greeted first, but a donkey. 'The first outlet for the pent-up enthusiasm came when that precious mascot made its appearance. Amos by name, this "mascot" can hardly be described as a thing of beauty, but it had been reported that he had been thrown out of the Everton ground, and this raised him to the height of something in the nature of a hero'.[10]

Postcard celebrating Barnsley's win over Everton,
FA Cup semi-final, 1910

Most of the players did arrive later in the evening, although it was rumoured that some got off at an earlier station, to avoid running the gauntlet of supporters. Those who stayed on the train until Barnsley were mobbed. 'Gadsby was seized upon, and half-a-dozen shoulders bore him along Eldon Street, whilst Bartrop and Glendenning ran off on their own, escaping what Tufnell hardly seemed to regard as an altogether comfortable position'.[11]

'Looker-On', a football reporter for the *Sheffield Daily Telegraph*, summed up the mood: 'Well, what do you make of it all? For the moment it seems impossible to fully grasp the significance of the position Barnsley have gained for themselves. English Cup Finalists!'[12] The ultimate prize, however, was still one step away. To win the cup Barnsley would have to overcome the mighty Newcastle United, at the time the most successful team in English football.

# Chapter 4

# Colliers and Magpies

The huge steel arch of the 'new' Wembley Stadium is now an impressive landmark visible for several miles across north London. There are some who doubt whether the new stadium will ever recapture the character of the original Wembley – frequently referred to as the spiritual home of English football. However, it should be remembered that the original Wembley Stadium did not open until 1923, more than fifty years after the first FA Cup competition was held. Many of the most exciting Cup Finals took place away from the twin towers of Wembley. Because England did not have a national stadium in those years, the Cup Final was moved between different grounds. For the first twenty years the Kennington Oval was the usual venue, until 1895 when the final was moved to a ground with much higher capacity – Crystal Palace. This is not to be confused with Selhurst Park, the current home of Crystal Palace FC, but rather their old football ground and now the site of the National Sports Centre athletics stadium.

For the three weeks leading up to the 1910 Cup Final, little else had been talked about in Barnsley. On the day of the match, the front page of the *Barnsley Chronicle* was devoted to the final, with profiles of every player, discussions and predictions from other newspapers (including papers from Newcastle) and critical analyses of the respective cup runs of the two teams. Since the final was to be played on 23 April, Shakespeare's birthday, the newspaper even printed a mock Shakespearean play on the topic. Bartrop's pre-match profile read as follows:

WILFRED BARTROP – Outside right. Born at Worksop. Age 21, height 5ft 8in., weight 11st. 12lbs. First season with Barnsley. Last season played for Worksop Town, and was in the Rest of the Midland League Team against the champions. A clever and speedy forward, who generally tries the soundest defence. Has a capital idea when to centre, and scores goals on his own. Can control the ball splendidly, and is good at corner kicks.[1]

With players like that, how could Barnsley fail? The Revd. Tiverton Preedy, one of the founders of Barnsley Football Club, certainly thought his team would be too good for Newcastle United. 'Our boys are simply going to smash 'em' said the quiet Reverend.

Why? Well, I've give you my reasons. In the first place, we have two backs who are unsurpassed throughout the length and breadth of the land. They seldom allow attacks to materialise. Our half back line is, I should say, better than that of almost any other First or Second Division team. Our outside-right and outside-left in the forward line are as fast on their feet as I want to see … well, we're going to smash Newcastle![2]

The local enthusiasm and Revd. Preedy's confidence were both summed up in a wonderful postcard produced ahead of the 1910 Cup Final. The Barnsley team are shown in front of the famous glass palace, with a legend perhaps only decipherable in South Yorkshire. 'Min, Ahm praad on yer, yov copped t'enemy's toffee. Naah yo mun Ever-ton or two o'coils thro' Newcastle, Captin Boyle, theer's Palace, leead on'. And so, on 23 April 1910, St. George's Day, two teams from the north of England travelled to London to compete in the 39th English Cup Final.

Most of the national press attention was focussed on Newcastle United. Although the club had won the league championship three times in recent years, they were the 'nearly men' when it came to the FA Cup. In the previous five seasons, they had reached the Cup Final a remarkable three times, yet had lost every one – and to a different club each time. Crystal Palace must have seemed an unlucky ground for the

Postcard produced ahead of the FA Cup Final 1910

most successful club in England. As for Barnsley, their supporters had never witnessed anything like this, and they travelled to the match in droves. The Midland, Great Northern, Great Central, and Lancashire and Yorkshire Railway Companies all ran special trains, some leaving Yorkshire late on the Friday night, and others as early as 1 a.m. on Saturday, thereby assuring the supporters of a truly full day in London. As *The Times* reported, 'dozens of excursion trains have travelled through the night with the holidaymakers and their stone jars of ale and pyramids of food'.[3] And according to their correspondent, it was not only food and drink that a Barnsley supporter brought, but also 'the lusty collier will bring "it" – that is to say, the girl he loves in his unemotional way'.[4] Seventy-seven thousand people, doubtless including 'it', packed into Crystal Palace providing gate receipts totalling almost seven thousand pounds.

The Barnsley team was composed of captain Tommy Boyle, goalkeeper Fred Mearns, Wilfred Bartrop on the right wing, plus Dickie Downs, Harry Ness, Bob Glendenning, George Utley, Harry Tufnell, George Lillycrop, Ernie Gadsby and Tom Forman. None of these players were well known outside the Barnsley area. Newcastle United, by comparison, included many familiar names, and a remarkable total of eight international players (a further two would pick up caps the following year). Colin Veitch, the captain, was the best known of the internationals, and one of the most popular sportsmen in England. Alongside him in the half-back line (midfield) played Scottish international Peter McWilliam and future international Wilf Low. Behind them in defence were big Irish international Billy McCracken and diminutive South African Tony Whitson, affectionately referred to as the 'long and short of it'.[5] In attack, prolific centre forward Albert Shepherd could rely on service from fellow England international John Rutherford on the right wing and Scotland's George 'Smiler' Wilson on the left. But above all, Newcastle United was a club concerned less about individuals and more about team work. As one writer put it: 'The most conspicuous factor of their success is combination. The Novocastrians are eleven enthusiastic units striving after one end. The majority of teams are eleven equally enthusiastic units striving after eleven ends'.[6]

Barnsley Football Club was fully aware of the gulf between the two outfits. The manager, directors and trainer put extra effort, therefore, into the physical preparation of the players. In the weeks leading up to the final, the team trained at Lytham St. Anne's in the northwest of England, as they had done before their other cup matches. Lytham was a seaside 'health resort', and it was felt that the invigorating sea air would help condition the men to the peak of fitness. Each morning, the training started with a cold plunge bath, followed by military style 'drills' based on a Swedish system of physical training. After a walk along the seashore, the men would then be taken through a series of long runs, short sprints, skipping, jumping and 'hard dancing' routines specially designed by trainer Bill Norman.[7] He was a tough taskmaster and, according to one who was put through the paces with the team, he could be 'a funny fellow when you didn't do as he told you'.[8] In the last few days before the Cup Final, practice with a football was barred, to reduce the chances of injury. Even heading practice was undertaken by jumping to head an imaginary football. The players were now ready for their toughest test.

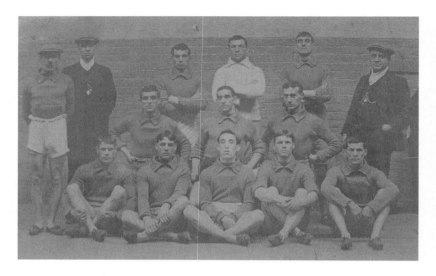

Cup tie training, Lytham St Annes, 1910
Players on back row (left to right): Downs, Mearns, Ness.
Middle row: Glendenning, Boyle, Utley. Front row: Bartrop, Gadsby,
Lillycrop, Tufnell, Forman.
Extreme left (standing): W. Norman, trainer

By kick-off on Cup Final Saturday the weather was fine, but with a
chilly wind causing many of the crowd to shiver with cold. As well as
the travelling supporters, various dignitaries from politics and the world
of football were present, plus special guests Viscount and Viscountess
Gladstone who arrived by motor car. Son of the former Liberal Prime
Minister, Gladstone had just stepped down as Home Secretary and was
now about to embark for South Africa as the Governor-General and
High Commissioner. Colin Veitch won the toss and Newcastle elected
to kick off with the wind and the sun to their backs. Despite the
difference in domestic achievements of the two teams, and the
supposed individual abilities of the players, the match was surprisingly
even. It was not, however, a classic by all accounts. Both teams, and the
referee, were criticised for the numerous stoppages of play, often due to
deliberate fouls or appeals for offside (usually against Bartrop) and other
infringements. The sight of defenders raising their arms to appeal to the

referee may seem a modern distraction, but this is clearly not the case, as one reporter at the match noted in classical analogy: 'Players on either side were constantly appealing with arms uplifted to the sky, as though they were members of a Greek chorus beseeching Zeus to hurl his thunderbolts'.[9]

Barnsley were not intimidated by their better known opponents, and as the first half drew to a close the team from Yorkshire took a surprise lead. Ernie Gadsby passed the ball to Bartrop who was running down the wing. As he reached the bye-line, he whipped in a cross from the right ('a fine inward pass', according to one report)[10] into the path of centre forward George Lillycrop. Rather than shooting, Lillycrop

Newcastle United captain Colin Veitch;
FA Cup Final Program 1910

cleverly dummied the ball, leaving it to run through to Harry Tufnell, whose quick reaction shot glanced in off the post. Against the odds, Barnsley FC were ahead. To score first against the acknowledged 'best team in England' gave a major boost to the Barnsley team. Speaking before the match, one anonymous 'football official' had even commented 'Barnsley's chance lies with getting a goal early, for if that happens the Newcastle players will begin arguing with each other, as usual'.[11]

In the second half, Barnsley came up with a new tactic. They had identified Tony Whitson as a possible weak spot on the left of the Newcastle defence, and so whenever possible the ball was spread wide to Wilfred Bartrop charging down the right flank. In fact, it was a tactic that one pundit had foreseen even before kick-off, writing 'Whitson will have one of the speediest wingers in Great Britain against him, and "Looker-On" expects to see Barnsley gaining a yard or two whenever Bartrop is given the ball'.[12]

Repeatedly Bartrop beat Whitson and crossed the ball into the penalty area, but big right-back Billy McCracken came across and nullified the threat every time. Newcastle responded to the tactic in a direct and heavy-handed way: Bartrop was heavily clattered by Wilf Low and had to leave the field for treatment. This shifted the balance of play in Newcastle's favour, and the Barnsley defence were now on the back foot. Dickie Downs, one of the Barnsley defenders, was particularly effective and earned effusive praise from *The Times'* reporter: 'Downs, the right back, struck one as a player of the very highest class who ought to have a good trial for England next year. He tackled admirably, and always disposed on the ball adroitly and to the advantage of his side. His kicking was brilliant in the extreme, some of his overhead kicks – put in when he was hotly pursued at full speed towards his own goal – being exhilarating to a degree'.[13]

As full time approached, the Newcastle United supporters could scarcely believe that their team were on the verge of losing their fourth Cup Final in six years. The Barnsley supporters were equally optimistic that, against all the odds, their team had triumphed in the ultimate cup competition. Mrs Ada Fairclough, wife of the manager Arthur Fairclough, untied the red ribbon from her umbrella so that she could adorn the FA Cup with the Barnsley club colours.[14] Then, in the 83rd minute, disaster struck for Bartrop's team. A long, high ball from midfield reached Jock Rutherford, the Newcastle outside right, who was sprinting forward. His looping header beat Fred Mearns in the Barnsley goal. Newcastle had equalized.

In the final few minutes, Newcastle United almost scored a winner, but after the regulation ninety the match ended a 1–1 draw. Viscount Gladstone could present neither the cup nor the medals, but he did give a short speech. He congratulated the two teams on their performances, regretted the lack of a definitive result, and said he hoped for an equally fair match in the next encounter. He also let slip his own allegiances, saying that 'perhaps his connection with Yorkshire might give him some bias towards Barnsley'[15] – a reference to his having been MP for Leeds for thirty years.

And so for the fifth time in history the FA Cup Final had to be replayed. There remain mixed views on the subject of replays. A replay is better than losing, of course, and for the club management it means substantially increased income from gate receipts. From a supporter's perspective, however, and a player's, there is a feeling of anticlimax: to have suffered the build-up of tension before the final, but without the emotional release that a result brings, whether that be winning or losing. Some of those waiting back at the Oakwell ground for the news to come through even declared 'they would rather Barnsley had lost outright'[16], instead of the anguish of a draw.[17]

Five days after the drawn game in London, the two teams – and over sixty thousand supporters – travelled to Goodison Park in Liverpool for the replay. This was an exceptional crowd for the Everton ground, which at the time had average gates of fewer than twenty thousand. The only other FA Cup Final to have been played there, in 1894, had attracted thirty-seven thousand spectators, so the attendance in 1910 was way beyond expectations. Just before the kick off, the swelling crowd broke through the barriers and spilled onto the pitch, and mounted police were needed to shepherd the people back into the stands before the game could begin. Portions of the crowd again overflowed after the match had started, but progressively the game developed without too much disruption.

It had been a wet few days in Liverpool, and the Everton pitch was in a poor and waterlogged state. Each drop of rain that morning was cheered by the travelling Barnsley supporters, who felt that the conditions might favour their team, or at least put a stop to the mesmerising passing game of the Newcastle United internationals. By kick off, however, the rain had stopped and the players ran out in bright sunshine to stand in the pools of water that had collected in the middle of the pitch. In fact, the conditions helped neither team, and many promising moves were aborted by poor control or misplaced passes. Wilfred Bartrop certainly took time to get used to the conditions. His initial contributions to the game were first to lose possession cheaply to McCracken, second to run the ball into touch before attempting his cross, and third to handle the ball when there was a great opportunity for an attack. His play improved as the match progressed, and on occasion his skill on the right wing earned a round of applause from the massive crowd.

But most of the talk on the terraces was not of Bartrop, it was of Newcastle United. It had been a narrow escape for the favourites in the first match at Crystal Palace, and from the outset it was clear that Newcastle United were adopting very different tactics for the replay. Barnsley FC had acquired a reputation as a physical side, with Newcastle famed for their fair play; but in this game the roles were reversed. The Magpies had decided it was time to get stuck in. Several ugly incidents ensued, as the *Daily Mirror* reported: 'Quite early on Higgins laid out Mearns rather badly, and when the Barnsley goalkeeper recovered he broke from the players who were supporting him and ran with clenched fists at Higgins, but was forcibly held back by the referee and Downs, his club mate'.[18]

The game was almost getting out of control. Barnsley right-back Dickie Downs, having acted as the peacemaker in that collision, was then himself the target of Newcastle aggression: 'Downs, who had played such a sturdy splendid game at Palace, was kicked. Thereafter Downs, although he played as sturdily as ever, limped badly'. Nor did his injury give him any immunity: 'Downs, who had been lamed in the first half, was lifted off his feet by a kick in the abdomen in the second half... Downs was laid out, and after he had been attended to, the other players held him up to see if he could stand but he collapsed altogether'.[19] No substitutes were permitted in football at that time; so, groggy and crippled, the Barnsley defender simply had to struggle on.

Perhaps Downs' heroic performance in the first match at Crystal Palace, complete with his acrobatic overhead kicks, had made Newcastle United single him out for closer attention in the replay. But there is a clear difference between close marking and physical violence, and many observers felt that the line had been crossed. By the end of the match shouts of 'Dirty Newcastle' were heard from all parts of the ground.[20] Their tactics were deplored, but it was also true that Newcastle United were the more skilful side.

The Newcastle players used the ball better in difficult, wet conditions, and outclassed Barnsley in both attack and defence. Veitch, Newcastle's captain, now appeared star of the show, stifling most of Barnsley's attacks and feeding precise balls to both wings. It was not all one-way traffic, however, and Barnsley could have gone ahead in the first half, through either Gadbsy or Bartrop – both had strong shots saved by Newcastle's long-serving goalkeeper Jimmy Lawrence. Then, six minutes into the second half, Albert Shepherd put Newcastle United ahead after a neat move started, as usual, by the captain. Veitch passed to Sandy Higgins, who threaded the ball between the Barnsley defenders. Shepherd raced through to slot it past Fred Mearns as he advanced out of goal.

Minutes later, Wilfred Bartrop had an excellent chance to equalise for Barnsley when he was put through on an open goal – but the winger fired a yard wide, whereupon 'a groan went up from the red and white supporters congregated in the enclosure'.[21] From this moment on, Newcastle United were firmly in the ascendancy. On their next attack their forwards got the ball into the net, only for the goal to be ruled out for both offside and handball! Then just a few minutes later, Albert Shepherd dribbled his way into the Barnsley penalty area, only to be brought down when the trio of Harry Ness, Dickie Downs and Harry Tufnell all piled in to block the shot. The referee promptly awarded a penalty kick, which was converted easily by Shepherd himself. Newcastle United could, and probably should, have scored again but they had already done enough. It had been a fantastic FA Cup run for Barnsley FC, but the team from the Second Division had been disappointed at the last.

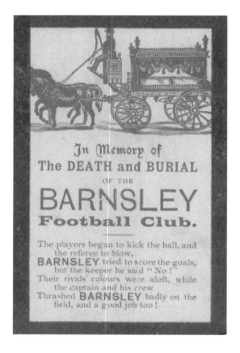

Unofficial memorial card produced in Newcastle following the
FA Cup Final, 1910
'The players began to kick the ball, and the referee to blow,
Barnsley tried to score the goals but the keeper he said "No!"
Their rivals' colours were aloft, while the captain and his crew
Thrashed Barnsley badly on the field, and a good job too!'

Bartrop and his team mates returned to Barnsley by train, arriving late in the evening. The team colours had been draped all around the town – houses, trams, people, dogs and horses – in hope of a victorious return. Even in defeat, however, large crowds waited for the team's train, which did not draw into the station until 11 p.m. Detonators had been placed on the track to signal the train's approach, which generated enthusiastic cheering from all those gathered. From the station the players were driven in a char-a-banc to the club's headquarters at the Clarence Hotel, followed by a huge crowd. Resisting the calls for speeches, the defeated and disappointed Barnsley team stayed inside. Their feelings were summed up by one player, who told a reporter: 'On today's play Newcastle were the better team, but we ought to have won on Saturday'.[22]

## Chapter 5

# Replays and replays

'I go, I go, look how I go, Swifter than the arrow from the Tartar's bow.'

So spoke Robin Goodfellow or Puck, the mischievous but friendly spirit of the woods, as he vanished swiftly into the forest in *A Midsummer Night's Dream*.[1] Shakespeare's words were also chosen to appear above the photograph of Wilfred Bartrop in a small book written about the Barnsley FC team in 1912, as being ideal to portray Bartrop's reputation as a fast and tricky winger. His skills on the right wing had played an important part in Barnsley's remarkable FA Cup run of 1910, and were to be pivotal again two years later.

Between 1910 and 1912, there were some significant changes to the Barnsley team. Goalkeeper Fred Mearns, who had saved a penalty in the 1910 semi-final and been clouted in the ill-tempered replay final against Newcastle United, was sold to Leicester Fosse, in part-exchange for a forward, George Travers. Even more controversial, however, was the sale of locally born captain Tommy Boyle to Burnley soon after the start of the 1911/12 season. A firm favourite with the supporters at Oakwell, Boyle was considered by many to be Barnsley's best player; indeed, he would later play for England. His place was taken by new recruit Phil Bratley, while Archie Taylor, another signing, took over the captain's responsibilities.

In the first round of the cup, played on 13 January 1912, Barnsley started with a 0–0 draw – a score line that would become very familiar to their supporters in the later rounds. Their opponents in that match were fellow Second Division side Birmingham City. Bartrop and his team mates dominated the replay, however, winning 3–0. This score was certainly a significant turn-around after the evenly matched fist game, but it appeared trivial compared to the achievement of Wolverhampton Wanderers in the same round. Wolves had drawn 0–0 with Watford in their first match, but then hammered the same team 10–0 in the replay!

In the second and the third rounds, Barnsley won without the need for replays. First, Leicester Fosse (later to become Leicester City) were beaten 1–0, then three weeks later Barnsley beat Bolton Wanderers 2–1 away. The Leicester match was one to remember for Wilfred Bartrop. Fifteen thousand supporters had walked through the snow to stand on the icy terraces at Oakwell. They witnessed an open, end-to-end game, but one littered with mistakes by both teams, each struggling on a frost-hardened pitch. Chances were spurned at each end, and just after the break Jack Cooper in the Barnsley goal saved a penalty. A few minutes later, Phil Bratley in the Barnsley defence pushed the ball forward to Bartrop, who broke away down the right wing. Faced with just the goalkeeper to beat, he sent in a fierce shot. Between the posts for Leicester was none other than Fred Mearns, Bartrop's former team mate who, just two seasons earlier, had helped Barnsley to reach the Cup Final. Mearns saved Bartrop's shot, but in the icy conditions he could not hold on to the ball. A good opportunist centre forward, George Lillycrop pounced and stabbed the loose ball home from close range.

In the quarter final, the Barnsley team were involved in one of the most remarkable matches in FA Cup history. They had drawn Bradford City, who were then the reigning FA Cup champions. This was a team to be feared, but also a glamour tie for Barnsley who were still in the Second Division. A souvenir postcard produced at the time gives a bemusing glimpse of the excitement that this match generated. The Barnsley players are depicted inside 11 balloons being pulled along on 11 strings by a small boy on a bicycle, with the caption 'And a little child shall lead them gently on their way'. The verse is from Isaiah 11:6, but here it was probably supplied by a 1909 silent film of the same name which was being screened in local theatres at the time of the match. The film had nothing to do with football, however.

Postcard produced before Barnsley's fourth round cup match
with Bradford City in 1912
Bartrop is inside the second balloon from the right on the middle row

The match was played at Oakwell on 9 March 1912, but Barnsley did not capitalise on their home advantage and a cautious game ended goalless. A replay at Valley Parade, home of Bradford City, took place four days later, and again no goals were scored. Today, a cup match would be settled by penalties after a drawn replay, but not in 1912. Instead, the teams were required to keep replaying the match until a winner was decided. The third match between the team was to be held at a neutral venue, and Elland Road, Leeds, was selected. This was a match full of incident and controversy, but alas not full of goals. The game witnessed several pitch invasions, the theft of £100 from the gate receipts, and finally abandonment of the match after 85 minutes, when the referee decided that the crowd encroachment was impeding play. The score at that point was again 0–0, and yet another replay was arranged. This time the venue was Bramall Lane, Sheffield.

The third replay was played on 21 March 1912, and produced the most exciting game of the cup campaign. Barnsley had been forced to make one change to their team, with 20-year old Jimmy Moore making his debut at outside left, to replace Bert Leavey who had suffered a broken leg in the abandoned match at Elland Road. The Barnsley team, therefore, was Jack Cooper in goal, Dickie Downs and Archie Taylor as fullbacks, Bob Glendenning, Phil Bratley and George Utley as half-backs, Jimmy Moore at outside left, Wilfred Bartrop at outside right, and Harry Tufnell, George Lillycrop and George Travers as inside forwards. New signing Travers scored for Barnsley, but Bradford fought back and equalised through Jimmy Speirs. Midfielder Archie Devine then put Bradford 2–1 ahead, and as full time approached it seemed that Barnsley FC were going out of the cup at the quarter-final stage. But with just five minutes of regular time remaining, George Lillycrop headed an equaliser and forced the match into extra time. After 29 minutes of extra time, no more goals had been scored and an astonishing fourth replay looked to be on the cards. With just seconds left Barnsley forced a corner, which Bartrop rushed over to take. He swung the ball into the Bradford City goalmouth, and in the ensuing melee Lillycrop stabbed the loose ball into the net. After seven hours of football, Barnsley had won with the last kick of the fourth match.

The two semi-finals were to be played at neutral venues. West Bromwich Albion and Blackburn Rovers would meet at Anfield in Liverpool, while the Barnsley team had a long journey south, to play Swindon Town at Stamford Bridge in London. Swindon Town were then in the Southern League, outside the Football League, so a win for Barnsley may have looked a formality. Yet such a view would be overlooking some important facts. First, Swindon were the reigning Southern League champions, whilst Barnsley had finished the 1910/11 season second from bottom in the English Second Division – the lowest tier of professional football. On paper this may look like two league positions between the teams. In fact, without provision for automatic relegation and promotion, the top non-league sides in 1912 were often more accomplished outfits than the lowest league teams. Second, Swindon Town's progress to the FA Cup semi-final was no fluke. They had reached the same stage in 1910 only to lose to Newcastle United (who had then beaten Barnsley in the final), and made the quarter-finals in 1911, losing to Chelsea. The amateurs of

Swindon Town also included one of the country's most prolific goalscorers – England international Harold Fleming. Equally importantly, this was a grudge match for the Barnsley team.

Swindon Town and Barnsley FC had last met on 5 May 1910, the day before the King's death, in a game played in the exotic location of the Vélodrome du Parc des Princes in Paris. After the end of the football season in England, the two teams had been invited to France to compete for the newly founded Dubonnet Cup. This competition was set up as an unofficial play-off between the FA Cup 'nearly men' – Barnsley who had lost to Newcastle United in the 1910 final, and Swindon who had lost to the winners in the 1910 semi-final. With a trophy at stake (an enormous ornate bronze vase valued at £40), the match was fiercely contested and the Barnsley team received criticism for their indisciplined approach. As the *Swindon Advertiser* reported: 'Barnsley played vigorous football, but completely lost their heads towards the finish'.[2]   By the final whistle, Swindon's international striker Harold Fleming had scored twice, in reply to one goal for Barnsley from George Lillycrop. Wilfred Bartrop and the rest of the Barnsley team, therefore, had to settle for a silver medal each, while the Swindon Town players were presented with impressive solid gold medals.[3] The largely French crowd of around five thousand enjoyed the spectacle, which also served to introduce the fast, hard-tackling nature of the English game to a country as yet without a professional league. As one French journal reported: 'It was a typical representation of the English national game… not an exhibition of football'.[4] Perhaps a seed was sown for improvement of the game in France, for the same article suggested that 'it was an admirable education for our players, who have seen how far one is able to go in the art of playing football'.[5]

Having lost the Dubonnet Cup to Swindon in 1910, the Barnsley players were determined not to suffer the same fate in the FA Cup in 1912. The semi-final was played on Saturday 30 March 1912, which turned out to be a dramatic day in the history of British sporting events for a quite different reason. At 11.40 a.m., the Oxford and Cambridge crews embarked from Putney on the 69th University Boat Race. The river conditions were atrocious, caused by a combination of strong

Barnsley FC and Swindon Town FC meet for the final of the
Dubonnet Cup in Paris, 1910

winds, a fast tide and heavy flood water. Huge crowds gathered in Putney, and all along the banks of the River Thames. After the first mile, with Oxford well in the lead, the Cambridge crew started to ship water, and as they reached Harrod's disaster struck as the light blue boat sank. The Oxford crew continued, but as they reached Hammersmith Bridge they too started to succumb to the rough water, and their boat sank at Chiswick. The Oxford crew did succeed in emptying and refloating their boat, and rowed to the finish, hoping to be crowned winners. To their dismay, the referee had already declared the contest a 'no race', and the crews were forced to race again two days later. Oxford would win the second contest, but the first was the only time in the history of the event that both boats have sunk.

The events on the Thames serve to emphasize the appalling weather conditions on that wet spring day in 1912. Wind and rain are usually enemies to skilful football, yet later that day two teams were to face each other in an FA Cup semi-final, just one-and-a-half miles from the Oxford and Cambridge sunken boats. At Stamford Bridge, the home ground of Chelsea, almost fifty thousand spectators gathered for the game, in which Barnsley fielded an unchanged side from their replayed replayed replay win over Bradford, including Wilfred Bartrop on the right wing.

In the first half, Swindon were by far the more attacking team and the Barnsley defenders were often forced to clear up-field in a state of panic. After the break, the Barnsley forwards started to work together and had several chances, including a fine shot from Bartrop which flew just the wrong side of the post. But the most significant event in an ultimately goalless draw involved Swindon Town's star striker Harold Fleming. He had been in remarkable form that season, having already scored 21 goals from 26 games in the league and cup. This, however, was to be Fleming's last game for Swindon Town for a considerable time. The Barnsley team were keenly aware of his goal threat. After all, it was his two strikes that had denied them the Dubonnet Cup in France two years previously. As a consequence, Fleming was subject to close marking and several hard challenges. In one of these, the Swindon striker received a knee to the groin that sent him crashing to the floor.

His injury turned out to be more serious than it first appeared: not only did he miss the last twenty minutes of the match – and the replay – but he remained invalided for the next ten months! Barnsley's vigorous tactics incurred the distaste of the London-based *Daily Express* which commented, with a clear regional bias, 'to stop a clever opponent by maiming him is not football as understood in the South'.[6]

After a few days of recuperation and training at Buxton, the Peak District spa town, the Barnsley players were ready for the semi-final replay. Because the first match had been played in London, much closer to Swindon than to Barnsley, it was only fair that the venue for the replay would be further north. The Football Association chose Meadow Lane, the ground of Notts County and just 30 miles from Bartrop's home town. In the first half, both teams had chances and Barnsley's Jack Cooper made another excellent penalty save to keep the scores level. On the hour mark the deadlock was finally broken, in a move that owed much to Wilfred Bartrop. George Travers headed against the crossbar, and Bartrop pounced on the rebounding ball. His shot was saved by Len Skiller, the Swindon Town goalkeeper, but he could only succeed in turning it around the post. Bartrop took the corner kick, which found Phil Bratley unmarked in the area. His headed goal sent the crowd wild and proved enough to seal the win for Barnsley.

After playing a total of ten games, five of which were goalless draws, Barnsley had again reached the English Cup Final. Six of the players remained from the 1910 team that were beaten finalists: Dickie Downs, Bob Glendenning, George Utley, Wilfred Bartrop, George Lillycrop and Harry Tufnell. Reaching two FA Cup Finals within three years, from outside the top flight of English football, was a remarkable achievement. Southampton – then a Southern League team – had done the same in 1900 and 1902, but had lost both finals. To improve on that record, Barnsley FC had to achieve just one thing: win the 1912 final.

## Chapter 6

# The 1912 Cup Final

According to a correspondent to *The Times*, there was one sure way to identify the uncouth Northerners descending upon London for the Cup Final: 'You may know them by the way they gaze at the legs of cab-horses'.[1] Every year from 1899 to 1912 at least one team in the Cup Final had been from the North of England, and was always accompanied by thousands of high-spirited visitors from Yorkshire, Lancashire, or the North-East, all heading for Crystal Palace. In 1910 it had been Barnsley and Newcastle, in 1911 Bradford and Newcastle, and in 1912 it was Barnsley again. This time their opponents were an accomplished First Division team from the Midlands: West Bromwich Albion.

There was a feeling among some observers that West Bromwich Albion was the more honourable team of the two – the team for the neutral to support. One reason was that the Albion had a reputation for developing home-grown talent, whereas few of the Barnsley players were actually from the town. The comparison was a little unfair, because although the Barnsley team included only two players from Yorkshire, a further four (including Bartrop) were from the neighbouring county of Nottinghamshire. A second reason for the neutral to back the Albion was that Barnsley had acquired a reputation as a very physical side. The manner in which Harold Fleming of Swindon Town had been dispatched in the semi-final appeared to confirm this. Not all observers agreed that a physical approach to the game was a bad thing, and certainly football in the pre-war years was a more vigorous and dangerous sport compared to today. Injuries to players were commonplace, partly because of the high-impact nature of the game and also because of the heavy boots then worn. Indeed, Barnsley had their own share of injuries during the 1912 Cup campaign and had lost their first choice outside left, Bert Leavey, when he had fractured his leg in two places during a collision with an opposing player. It should also be recalled that Barnsley had lost the 1910 Cup Final to a very physical, indeed aggressive, Newcastle United side.

The final was held on Saturday 20 April 1912, which turned out to be a beautiful spring day. The *Daily Mirror* gave a lyrical description of the Cup Final weather: 'The afternoon was delightfully fine, the sun blazing forth from a blue sky, flecked by the whitest of clouds, and a gentle breeze just tempering the fierceness of its rays'.[2]

Crystal Palace was now the regular Cup Final venue, and the ground where Barnsley and Newcastle United had met in 1910. Previous finals had shown that Crystal Palace could cope with truly massive crowds, with almost a hundred and fifteen thousand present when Tottenham Hotspur and Sheffield United drew in 1901, and over one hundred thousand when Aston Villa beat Newcastle United fours years later. Between seventy and eighty thousand was the usual expectation. Not all of the crowd could actually see the game – many thousands of fans would have caught only glimpses of play – but all were part of the Cup Final experience.

*The Times* had predicted a huge crowd again, arguing that 'The Barnsley collier will even sell his terrier to buy a ticket for the Final Cup-tie'.[3] The prediction was wrong. The 1912 final drew the smallest attendance at a Cup Final for fifteen years: a mere fifty-five thousand. The reason was not that the two teams were based far from London; after all, this was the norm – it had been more than two decades since the Cup Final included a London club. The real reason was almost certainly financial. Throughout the spring of 1912, miners throughout the country had walked out as part of a national strike over pay; full union members were now trying to struggle by on just 10 shillings a week. As one reporter put it: 'Evidently the coal strike had affected the contents of the "pot dog", or earthenware ornament, which graces the mantelpiece of so many Northern living rooms, and is commonly used as a savings bank'.[4] The same writer also noted that 'the railway companies had not been so liberal as in former years to Cup-tie excurtionists'. Consequently, a large proportion of the crowd were not from Barnsley, or indeed West Bromwich, but were neutral observers from the London area.

The atmosphere throughout the match was subdued, as *The Times* reported: 'Although the play was always good and at times really brilliant, each side getting a grip of their characteristic game from the start and keeping it to the end, the crowd was seldom moved to enthusiasm, and regular attendants at these annual carnivals of professional football were puzzled to account for the lethargy which suggested, as one of them pointed out, that nobody cared a brass button about the result of the match'.[5]

But it was not the heat, or the coal strike, that was affecting the mood of the crowd. The explanation was more tragic. For the week leading up the match, the newspapers had been dominated by one event: the sinking of the *Titanic*. Just six days earlier, a little before midnight, the largest passenger ship in the world had struck an iceberg on its maiden voyage between England and America. The first newspaper reports in England suggested there were no casualties, but as the week wore on the true horror gradually emerged. By Saturday morning, it was clear that over fifteen hundred passengers and crew had lost their lives in the worst maritime disaster the country had ever seen. The country was in shock.

One newspaper reporter who mixed with supporters before and after the game commented: 'There can be no doubt that there was another and nobler thought in the corporate mind of the great assemblage. People could not help thinking and talking about the *Titanic* catastrophe. In the trains, both going and returning, the writer found himself in the company of Northern enthusiasts who in ordinary circumstances would have been talking football. But they were looking at the evening papers and commenting on the new facts disclosed by the survivors of the ship wreck'.[6]

A remarkable silent film has survived that shows the opening sequence of the match. Discovered on the floor of the Palace Picture House in Edinburgh after it had closed down in the 1930s, and long thought to be a clip of Leith Athletic[7], the fragment of newsreel was not correctly identified until 1999. In the film, the West Bromwich Albion players emerge first from the tunnel, striding purposefully onto the pitch, flanked by police. The Barnsley captain Archie Taylor emerges next, alongside goalkeeper Jack Cooper pulling on his leather gloves, with the rest of the team jogging out behind. The muscular figure of Wilfred Bartrop is easily spotted, the fourth of the Barnsley players to emerge, with a steely look on his face. The players and kit do not look very different from those seen at any match up to the 1950s, but the same cannot be said for the referee! Wearing long shorts, below jacket, waistcoat and tie, plus a hat, Mr Schumacher hardly seemed dressed for 90 minutes of running and officiating.[8]

Wilfred Bartrop, centre of the picture, emerging from the tunnel for the 1912 FA Cup final at Crystal Palace

The two teams contesting the Final had very different pedigrees, and quite contrasting styles. West Bromwich Albion were known as a particularly skilful side, relying on short, accurate passing, possession football and a patient build-up to their attacks. Barnsley had several fast, strong players, who preferred to get the ball forward quickly, if not always accurately. They had also been criticised for their rugged methods in some previous matches. Yet as the match developed, it soon became clear that the Barnsley players had tempered the physical side of their game for the Cup Final. Had they gone too far? The *Daily Mirror* certainly thought so, complaining that that Barnsley 'played a namby pamby sort of game'.[9] The reporter from *The Times,* by contrast, still condemned the 'rough-and-ready Barnsley men'.[10]

During the first half of the final, the First Division team was dominant and the Barnsley defence was hard pressed. Archie Taylor and Dickie Downs both made key interceptions to stop goal-scoring chances, and Jack Cooper was forced to make two vital saves. After the break,

West Bromwich Albion, in the pale stripes, kick off in
the 1912 FA Cup final at Crystal Palace

however, the Barnsley midfield and forwards began to click, and the West Bromwich defence was now the one struggling. *The Times* reporter was impressed by 'Bartrop's speedy runs down the right wing',[11] while the *Daily Mirror* described him as 'nearly the best forward on the field'.[12] But although Bartrop's crosses caused West Bromwich trouble, their goalkeeper Hubert Pearson repeatedly came to the rescue, as did both the crossbar and the upright. Overall, the finishing of the forwards on both sides was woeful, and it was the two defences that stood out. Jesse Pennington in the Albion defence was one of those in sterling form. As one reporter commented, 'With what certainty he tackled Bartrop, and with what unerring touch he kept the ball in play and placed to his forwards!'[13] A 0–0 scoreline at full time was judged a fair result.

For the third year in a row, the FA Cup final had ended in a draw, and a replay became necessary.[14] The Barnsley supporters had experienced the anticlimax of a drawn cup final before, in 1910, and the general feeling was summed up by the *Sporting Chronicle*:

> Everyone is sorry that for three years in succession the final has borne so much resemblance to the chapter in a serial that lures and leads to an exciting situation, and then says: "To be continued in our next". The final is worse than this, because when we take our fiction in homeopathic doses we expect linked plotting long drawn out, but when folks travel hundreds of miles at considerable expense to see the last scene of all that ends this eventful tournament, they ought not to be denied the chance of a legitimate conclusion without some effort on the part of the players.[15]

Yet by forcing a replay, the Barnsley team now had a significant advantage. For the first and only time in FA Cup history, the Final would be replayed in Yorkshire, close to the club's bedrock of support. The venue was Bramall Lane, the ground on which Barnsley had achieved their last-gasp comeback against cup-holders Bradford City in the fourth round. For Wilfred Bartrop, this was almost a home tie: Worksop is just 20 miles from Sheffield. He could be guaranteed that his large extended family and numerous friends would make the short journey to support their local star. Among them, and possibly the most important, was 22-year old Ruby Millership, Wilfred's girlfriend.

Wednesday 24 April 1912 was another hot and sunny day. The roads to Sheffield were filled with bicycles and char-a-bancs carrying local supporters, and the trains were also crowded. Hundreds of men and boys, 'adorned with red ribbons', even decided to walk, although several regretted the decision later: 'One enthusiast frankly confessed that his calculation of saving the railway fare from Barnsley to Sheffield was wrong, adding that lubrication – internal application – had proved more expensive'.[16]

Nevertheless, the attendance was lower than expected: only 38,555. Part of the reason was that this was a mid-week match and few working men could absent themselves legitimately. In addition, money was still in short supply in the aftermath of the coal strike. The Bramall Lane pitch was dry and hard, unusually so for the time of year, with several bare patches comprising just dirt and dust. The conditions made for a fast-paced game in which close control of the ball was difficult, but both sides carved out shooting opportunities. In the first half, West Bromwich Albion started by far the brighter, and the Barnsley goalkeeper Jack Cooper was called upon within the first few minutes. As the half wore on, however, Barnsley started to get a grip of the game and mounted several swift attacks towards the Albion goal. As one witness recounted:

> Bartrop was a bold figure in these raids. Once he drove the ball on the ground in front of the goal mouth, but there was too much pace in his boot, and none of the other forwards could get near to the quickly moving object. Bartrop and his mates continued the pressure, but the Yorkshiremen were never allowed to make a shot, and if Pearson occasionally fielded the ball he never had a troublesome situation – save one caused by his own mistake when he failed to parry a high centre from Bartrop. Even then Travers could not get a shooting position, and Moore was wide of the mark.[17]

In the second half, Barnsley stepped up the pace even more, and came close to scoring on several occasions. They also got a little carried away at times, and were spoken to by the referee 'for an excess of zeal'.[18] Bartrop was again in the thick of the action, both in his wing play and in front of goal where he missed a good chance. At the opposite end, Bob Glendenning was involved in an unusual incident, which still has repercussions to this day. At one point West Bromwich Albion looked certain to score, but Glendenning, who was off the field receiving treatment, suddenly raced back onto the pitch and cleared the ball from the goal line, while wearing just one boot. This was perfectly within the rules in 1912, but it had clearly prevented a Cup Final goal for West Bromwich Albion. Nowadays, FIFA Law 4 stipulates that no player can re-enter the field of play without the referee being satisfied that he has 'corrected his equipment'. Ninety-four years after the Glendenning incident, in a World Cup qualification match between England and Azerbaijan in 2006, David Beckham raced back onto the pitch, again wearing just one boot. In this case, the assistant referee was all too familiar with FIFA Law 4, and Beckham received a yellow card for his troubles.

As a result of the Glendenning incident, the match was still goalless after 90 minutes, and because this was a replay, half an hour extra time was to be played. During the short interval while the teams changed ends and caught their breath, players from the two Sheffield-based teams, Sheffield United and the Wednesday, mingled with the crowd, collecting money for the *Titanic* Disaster Fund. Some had commented that a collection should have been held during the final at Crystal Palace, but at least football had belatedly found its charitable side. That the collections were made by the actual players of the two local professional teams, rather than officials or other volunteers, also speaks for the feeling of the country at the time. A total of £49 was collected. Although this appears a small sum, particularly considering that the gate receipts were £2,615, many spectators will have stretched their meagre budgets to near breaking point in order to attend the game.

The match was finely balanced, and the standard of play judged to be higher than in the previous meeting at Crystal Palace. Forwards from both teams created many opportunities, while both sets of defenders also showed their class, most notably Downs for Barnsley and Pennington for West Bromwich Albion. Wilfred Bartrop was also singled out for some effusive praise:

> No forward on either side showed such strength and speed combined as Bartrop. He had a long duel with Pennington, and save for one attempted trip he was chivalrous to his old opponent. These two have had many tussles, and I cannot pay Bartrop a higher compliment than to say that the match was drawn. Bartrop is a long-striding wingman, with rare powers to place his centres, but he was magnificently served by Tufnell, who was most persevering, and often dainty and elusive in his footwork.[19]

The tussle between Bartrop and Pennington may have been drawn, but the Cup final replay was not. After 28 minutes of extra time, just two minutes before the final whistle, came the most dramatic moment of the afternoon. A single goal, a cup-winning goal, conjured out of nothing. It had taken three-and-a-half hours of Cup Final play, if the meeting at Crystal Palace is also counted, to break the deadlock. And when the cup-winning goal came, it was firmly against the run of play. Albion were laying siege to the Barnsley goal and looked certain to score, but Barnsley were resolute in their defending. The Barnsley half-back Bob Glendenning controlled the ball, beat two attacking players, and cleared as far as Harry Tufnell, who was standing close to the half-way line. Tufnell set off on an electrifying run towards the Albion goal. After beating Arthur Cook, there was now just one defender with a chance to stop the Barnsley forward reaching the Albion goal. That man was Jesse Pennington – England international and captain of West Bromwich Albion. 'Fair in complexion and conflict, debonair and dashing',[20] Pennington was widely known as a 'gentleman of the game'. Now he had a clear opportunity to bring Tufnell down but, with his unshakable sense of fair play, Pennington declined and Tufnell raced through unimpeded. Hubert Pearson, the Albion goalkeeper advanced in an attempt to block the shot, but Tufnell calmly slotted the ball to one side. Barnsley supporters swarmed onto the pitch, and Harry Tufnell was enveloped by the crowd.

Ivan Sharpe, a former England amateur player present in the crowd, described it as the greatest goal he had ever seen. His description is wonderful:

> On he goes – 10, 20, 30 yards ... one eye on right-back Cook's race to outflank him; the other eye on goalkeeper Pearson's advance to narrow the angle. With every stride, the strategic situation alters. And all amid a screaming pandemonium. Should he shoot? If so, when? Should he slip the ball past the goalkeeper and try to follow? He shoots ... and there is the ball sailing towards the net with the goalkeeper helplessly turning on his haunches to see his dream of a medal disappear.[21]

It was to be the last significant action of the match. For Barnsley Football Club, it was their finest moment, and for six of the players – including Wilfred Bartrop – the disappointment of 1910 was practically erased. They were the English Cup winners.

As the news filtered through to Barnsley, a huge and jubilant crowd began to build up in the streets, waiting for the return of the victorious team.[22] The first arrivals from Sheffield were some of the supporters who had been lucky enough to go to the game; and cheers from the crowd greeted the arrival of each weary returning cyclist. At 8.45 p.m., the char-a-banc carrying the Barnsley team appeared, setting off wild scenes. People swarmed around the vehicle, with many climbing onto the sides as it drove slowly through the crowd behind mounted police. The famous trophy was displayed at the front of the bus, and each member of the team was cheered in turn. The players responded by waving their hats in appreciation. Behind the team's char-a-banc there followed a procession of cars carrying supporters, and each of these was also mobbed, with people hanging onto their sides. The raucous procession reached the Clarence Hotel, the headquarters of Barnsley Football Club, and speeches were made from a second storey balcony by the Mayor and by several of the players. Nobody could hear a word, and nobody cared that they had not.

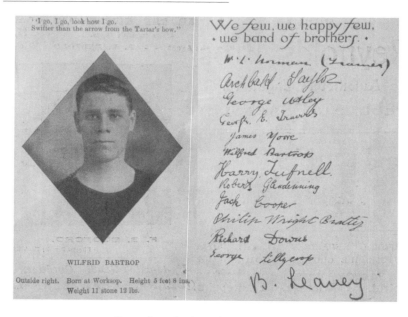

Pages from 'Lifting the Cup' 1912

The FA Cup winning team, 1912
Back row: Downs, Cooper, Taylor.
Second row: Norman (trainer), Bartrop, Bratley, Moore, Hastie (Secretary).
Seated: Glendenning, Lillycrop, Utley. On ground: Tufnell, Travers.
Inset is Griffin who signed after the Cup win

The FA Cup trophy paraded by open-top bus
Bartrop is third from right

FA Cup winner's medal awarded to Wilfred Bartrop

## Chapter 7

# The girl next door

'Posh and Becks' were the ultimate celebrity couple for the end of the twentieth century. The marriage between an England international footballer and a member of one of the most successful pop groups of the 1990s guaranteed incessant media coverage of their lives. But perhaps there really is nothing new under the sun. Almost a century ago, Colin Veitch, who had captained Newcastle United in the 1910 Cup Final win over Barnsley, and an England international like Beckham, was likewise half of a celebrity couple. His second marriage was to a professional actress, Greta Burke, who had appeared in several productions staged by Veitch's own theatre company, the People's Playhouse. The couple were certainly not shy and retiring, and were said to perform *Romeo and Juliet*, using the balcony of their Newcastle house, while the neighbours looked on. Veitch was a cultured, even scholarly, man with an active interest in the arts, politics and education. He was a patron of the Newcastle Operatic Society, an active member of the socialist *Clarion* movement, and a friend of playwright George Bernard Shaw. He had been offered the post of headmaster at a school and he had been asked to stand as a parliamentary candidate on two occasions.[1]

Wilfred Bartrop's life was very different. The son of a worker at a timber yard and brewery, and raised in a mining community, he moved in very different circles to Colin Veitch. On 6 August 1912, just three and a half months after becoming an FA Cup winner, Wilfred married Ruby Emily Millership. Ruby was, quite literally, the girl next door. Wilfred's mother and father had lived at many addresses in Worksop, and around

1910 they had moved into 17 Clinton Street on the south-eastern edge of town. Wilfred was no longer living permanently with the family, as he now played his football for Barnsley FC, but he was a regular visitor to his parents' house. And one person who did not escape his notice was Ruby, who was two years younger and living in the adjacent terraced house, number 15. She had been born in Islington, London, in 1889, the second child of a grocer's assistant, Augustus Millership, and his wife Emily. The family moved several times between London and the Midlands, but tragically her father died when Ruby was still a young child. By 1901, Ruby had settled in Worksop, together with her sister Ivy, brothers Frank and Hubert, and mother Emily, who meanwhile had married Charles Stringfellow, a coal miner originally from Stafford.

Ruby Millership with elder brothers Frank (right) and Hubert (left)

The marriage between Ruby and Wilfred took place at the Registry office in Worksop and was witnessed by one of Wilf's sisters, Elsie May Bartrop, and by Ruby's stepfather. The groom's occupation is given quite clearly as 'Professional Football Player'. But perhaps the most intriguing parts of the certificate were the mistakes made on it, and the corrections! The Registrar very clearly first entered the name 'Wilfred Charles Henry Bartrop', and then made two alterations to switch this to the true name 'Charles Henry Wilfred Bartrop'. Since Wilfred never used his full name, perhaps his sister had to remind him on the big day; or maybe the Registrar was simply awestruck and set down the name 'Wilfred', by which he was publicly known, when Worksop's current sporting hero, and recently crowned FA Cup winner, declared his intention to get married.

Wilfred was still playing for Barnsley FC at the time of the marriage, and so Ruby moved to Barnsley to join her new husband. Several years later the couple would move back into Worksop, this time to Allen Street – a row of newly built, neat terraces with small front gardens. This

Marriage between Wilfred Bartrop and Ruby Millership

was a fashionable part of town, close to the town centre, with a recently opened billiards hall at the end of the street and two theatres around the corner. Coincidentally, the street was named after William Allen, the former President of Worksop Town Football Club, for whom Wilfred had played at the start of his football career. Unfortunately, the house at which they lived, number 12, no longer exists because the even-numbered houses on the street were demolished to make way for the bus station in 1977. Wilfred and Ruby Bartrop were probably quite comfortably off. The maximum wage for professional footballers was £5 at the time, although not every player earned this much, and Barnsley FC were paying most of the team around £3 per week. This was not a princely sum, but it was still double the amount earned by manual workers and coal miners, who will have made up a substantial part of the home crowds for Barnsley's matches.

On top of whatever basic salary Wilfred earned, clubs were also allowed to pay bonuses – and these were sometimes substantial. For example, under Football Association rules, Barnsley FC was permitted to distribute a total of £275 between the players, as a cup winners' bonus. Wilfred Bartrop received £25, as did most of the other players. Bert Leavey, who had broken his leg in a tackle midway through the campaign, received only £12 10s, as clearly he had not contributed quite as much to the team effort! Young Jimmy Moore who had replaced Leavey in the team, and picked up a cup-winners' medal, received the same 'half bonus'. New rules capping the level of bonus had just come into force; indeed, two years earlier the players had fared even better. In 1910, as beaten finalists, each player had received the huge bonus of £100. Successful clubs could, generally, afford such sums. For example, in 1912 Barnsley FC received over £8000 from gate receipts for the FA Cup run alone.

For Wilfred, the £125 banked from FA Cup bonuses in was supplemented by extras earned from foreign tours and invitation matches. For example, the Dubonnet Cup in Paris, against Swindon Town, may have attracted only five thousand spectators, but it was financed by a rich entrepreneur and the clubs (and players) would certainly have benefited financially. This match was the first in an

A dapper looking Wilfred Bartrop around 1912

extensive continental tour made by Barnsley FC, lasting for almost a month in 1910. After Paris, the team played invitation matches in Germany, Austria and finally Hungary, playing more than ten games altogether, including three in three days in Budapest! Furthermore, they won almost all of these matches, apart from the initial Dubonnet Cup and one game against Ferencváros. The tour included matches against some well-known European sides. Wiener Sportclub of Austria (whom Barnsley beat 5–3) is Vienna's oldest and most famous Athletics Club; Gratz of Austria were beaten 12–2, while Ferencváros of Budapest were the Hungarian league champions, a title they had won five times in the previous eight years. One of their matches in Vienna, which Barnsley won 3–1, was particularly memorable for the fact that the referee walked off at half-time and refused to continue because of the unruly nature of the crowd. The match could only be completed when a sufficiently brave substitute official had been found![2]

The Barnsley team in Budapest, summer 1910
Back row (left to right): Downs, Glendenning, Mearns, Boyle, Ness, Utley.
Front row: Bartrop, Gadsby, Lillycrop, Tufnell, Forman

The Cup Final win of 1912 had been a remarkable achievement, but the club was still in the Second Division of English football. Promotion was now the clear goal of the management and the players. Over the next few years, this remained just out of reach, as the players struggled to find consistency, notwithstanding some impressive performances. George Utley had been in such good form that he was selected to play for England, while Dickie Downs came close to being chosen to represent the Football League.[3] Problems on the field were compounded by financial difficulties that started to trouble the club, as a result of which players had to be sold. To the dismay of supporters, the FA Cup winning team of 1912 was gradually broken up. Within a year of their victory, Bob Glendenning was sold, and in the following season Bert Leavey, George Lillycrop and international George Utley were all transferred to other clubs. Their replacements were not generally considered to be of the same calibre; as one season ticket-holder complained, 'It has been like paying for strawberries and cream, and being served with gooseberries and skimmed milk'.[4]

As for the cup-winning players still remaining at the club, future success with Barnsley must now have seemed an increasingly unlikely prospect. In February 1914 another of the medallists was sold, George Travers going to Manchester United. Next, it proved to be Wilfred Bartrop's turn. On 25 April 1914, five thousand spectators at Analby Road watched Barnsley beat Hull City 1–0, the goal being scored by Harry Tufnell from a Wilfred Bartrop corner kick.[5] He did not know it then, but this was his last competitive game for Barnsley Football Club. A new club secretary had taken over, Percy Lewis, formerly with Stockport County.[6] By early May most of the team had been re-signed, but Bartrop's name was absent from the list. In the middle of that month, it was announced that he had been transferred.

Ironically, therefore, many of the 1912 FA Cup winners achieved their ambition of playing in the First Division, but it was not with Barnsley. The medallists were now spread between many of the top clubs in English football, including Manchester United, Bolton Wanderers, Sheffield United and – for Wilfred Bartrop – Liverpool Football Club.

## Chapter 8

## Scandal at Liverpool

Moving to a bigger club and playing at a higher level can be a mixed blessing for a professional footballer. In today's game the attractions can include higher salaries and, for some, the chance to qualify for and play in European club competitions. Ninety years ago, these were not the primary considerations. There was a maximum wage payable to footballers, so moving to a higher level did not always make a big difference. Much depended on how generous the former club had been (or how far the rules could be bent). Formal, annual European club competitions were then non-existent, so that was not a relevant consideration. The attraction of moving from a Second to a First Division club was, therefore, largely about pride, prestige and progression: the chance to be part of a stronger team, to play alongside better players, to compete against the bigger clubs in front of bigger crowds. The higher profile would also increase the chance of being picked to represent your country.

But there have always been downsides. The bigger clubs have the luxury of larger squads, so breaking into the team is a challenge. Today there are many cases of apparently outstanding players transferring to a bigger, richer club, yet not making the first team – established internationals sitting on the substitutes' bench, or playing for the reserve team. The problem was even more acute 90 years ago. There were reserve teams, and these often played in front of reasonable crowds; but there was generally little rotation of players. Breaking out of the reserves and into the first team was difficult. Because the Football Association rules stipulated that a club must always play its strongest side in first-team games, it was generally only injury or abysmal form that opened the way for a reserve team player. The biggest difference from today was that for almost the first century of the professional game there was no substitutes' bench. It was not until 1965 that substitution of players became permitted in league games, and even then only in the event if an injury. In Bartrop's day, the eleven players picked to start the game were the eleven players to end the game – if they were all still standing. There was no chance for tactical changes, no way to replace an injured player, and no opportunity to bring on fresh legs. A manager could not try out a newly signed player for the last 15 minutes, perhaps as a stepping stone towards a regular team place. A footballer was not aiming to be part of the 'starting eleven'; he had to aim simply to be one of the eleven.

Wilfred Bartrop was signed by First Division club Liverpool FC on 13 May 1914. The *Liverpool Echo* reported the signing with great enthusiasm under the buoyant headline 'Barnsley Brilliants Bought for Anfield'.[1] Liverpool Football Club had acquired the signatures of not one but two of Barnsley's FA Cup winners. Centre half Phil Bratley had been on Barnsley's transfer list at his own request, and was therefore easily acquired by the Reds. But Wilfred Bartrop was another matter altogether. At first, Barnsley were reluctant to release the pacy winger, and after Liverpool had shown their interest the negotiations dragged on. Eventually, £900 was paid to secure the two players' signatures, and so Bratley and Bartrop moved to Liverpool ready for the 1914/15 season.

At Barnsley, Wilfred Bartrop had been the first choice for the outside right position – the attacking right winger – for five seasons. It was for this position, number seven on the team sheet, that he was signed by Liverpool's manager Tom Watson. Bartrop was described in the Liverpool press as 'an outside right with a burst of speed'.[2] He could look forward to an exciting year. He already had an FA Cup winner's medal, and now he was part of one of the biggest clubs in England, playing in the First Division. Several of his new team mates were established or rising stars, and included the future England captain Ephraim Longworth. The Liverpool captain, Harry Lowe, was born just outside Worksop, so there was even a geographical connection. Unbeknown to Bartrop, however, his glory days were over. Twin forces would now conspire against him – bad timing and a bad apple.

The timing problem was catastrophic, not just for football but for the world. On 28 June 1914, just seven weeks after Bartrop's transfer, Archduke Franz Ferdinand, heir to the Austro-Hungarian throne, was assassinated in Sarajevo. This precipitated chaos in Europe. Austria–Hungary declared war on Serbia, whose ally Russia mobilised forces in defence. Germany, allied to Austria-Hungary, declared war on Russia on 1 August and on France, bound by treaty to Russia, on 4 August. On the same day, Germany invaded Belgium on route to Paris. Britain, a guarantor of Belgian independence, declared war on Germany.

Despite the outbreak of hostilities, the 1914/15 football league season started as normal and Liverpool played their first match on 2 September, against Bolton Wanderers at Anfield. Liverpool won 4–3, but neither Bartrop nor his former Barnsley team-mate Bratley had been selected. League matches continued and of the next ten games, through September and October 1914, Liverpool drew two, lost five and won three. Bratley succeeded in breaking into the team, and played in both their worst defeat and their best win of the season: a 5–0 defeat to Everton away and a 7–2 home win over Tottenham Hotspur. Bartrop was yet to make an appearance.

The bad apple was Bartrop's competitor for the Liverpool number seven position: Jackie Sheldon. In the 1914/15 season, Liverpool FC had a huge squad and used a total of 22 different players during the league campaign: Sheldon, Bartrop, Campbell, Longworth, Pursell, Lowe, Ferguson, Metcalfe, Miller, Lacey, Nicholl, Speakman, Banks, McDougall, Bratley, McKinlay, Pagman, Crawford, Hafekost, Scott, Wadsworth and the superbly named Fairfoul. The use of so many players might seem an early example of the rotation system, but was more likely a reflection of disruption caused by the war. By all accounts, Jackie Sheldon was an outstanding player. He had signed for Liverpool only six months before Bartrop, from Manchester United, and quickly established himself as Liverpool's favoured outside right. Sheldon scored in the first home game of the 1914/15 season and then again in the first away game, this time from the penalty spot. Over the course of the 1914/15 season, he scored 10 goals, a tally exceeded only by Tom Miller and Frederick Pagnam. But the last named had an exceptional strike rate – Pagnam's 24 league goals scored that season came in just 29 matches, and he even allowed Sheldon to take the penalties!

Wilfred Bartrop had to wait for three months before getting his chance in the first team. Liverpool had gone six matches without a win, and Sheldon was experiencing a barren patch, having not scored since October. On 19 December 1914, manager Tom Watson selected Bartrop to play in a home match against the league leaders Oldham Athletic. The weather was atrocious, with torrential rain throughout the afternoon. The centre of the pitch and both penalty areas turned into muddy quagmires. Many spectators stayed away because of the rain and so the newly built Kop (the 'Spion Kop' to give its full name), which was uncovered in those days, was almost deserted. For those Liverpool fans who did brave the conditions, the cold and wet day quickly turned worse. Within a minute of the kick off, Oldham Athletic went a goal ahead, having scored through a thirty yard screamer from Gilbert Kemp. For a time the Liverpool team were stunned, and struggled to get back into the game. They did find their form later in the first half, and Bartrop on his First Division debut was at the centre of several moves that came close to providing an equaliser. First, he 'drove across a lovely ball'[3] from the right wing towards Fred Pagnam in front of goal, but the usually clinical striker lost his footing and missed the ball completely. The same happened a little later, when Bartrop fired in a powerful cross towards Jimmy Nicholl. Clearly the muddy ground was proving a severe handicap to the strikers. Keeping the ball in the air avoided some of the problems, and midway through the first half Bartrop tried to score with a weighted lob over one of Oldham's tall defenders. This time goalkeeper Howard Matthews was well positioned and tipped the ball over the crossbar for a corner. Not all Bartrop's efforts were quite so threatening, and one reporter was particularly critical about a promising run that ended with a very poor cross, when 'a centre to Nicholl must have meant a goal'.[4]

In the second half, Pagnam did manage to equalise for Liverpool with a delicate flicked header from a Billy Lacey cross, and the game seemed to be heading for a draw. But with four minutes remaining, the league leaders conjured up a winner out of nothing. Oldham's centre-half Elliot Pilkington managed to control the ball for a long mazy dribble, through the cloying mud, and slotted the ball home from just two yards. For the Liverpool team, it was a disappointing end to a scrappy game, and one that gave the local sports reporters much to grumble about. 'When all else fails, blame the referee' is a common reaction in football, and this was also true in 1914. Under the banner 'Curious refereeing', the *Liverpool Football Echo* started the complaints with an observation: 'The referee, by the way, is a disciple of the sect that carries the whistle in the mouth for the whole of the game'.[5]

Mr Sharpe was also keen to be seen to be in charge of proceedings; even if this meant being likened to 'an arrogant scarecrow defying a cheeky sparrow'.[6] This all contributed to the stop-start nature of the game, with the stops much too frequent for the newspaper reporters' liking and usually at unfortunate moments (from a Liverpool perspective). Numerous questionable offsides were given, but then the offside rule was one 'for which he has peculiar interpretation'.[7] Physical contact between players was much more accepted in 1914 than it is today, indeed was considered part of the game; hence the *Echo* reporter's outrage that the Liverpool striker Fred Pagnam was penalised for a shoulder charge (a 'nudge') on one of the Oldham defenders. The armchair advice now dispensed was for Pagnam not to hold back on account of one fussy referee – others would be more lenient: 'Keep it up Pagnam, it will often carry you through. Besides, get your blow in first and you can score at your leisure while the full-back picks himself up!'[8]

Wilfred Bartrop's debut had not been a great success, but nor was it a disaster. His team had lost very narrowly to the First Division leaders, which appeared no cause for disgrace. There had been weaknesses in communication between Bartrop and the other forwards, and also between Bartrop and Billy Lacey who was playing behind him on the right wing; but this was understandable considering it was his first match alongside most of the team. Some positives could be taken from the game. Bartrop had been at the heart of many of Liverpool's attacking moves and it was his runs down the right wing that had resulted in several dangerous crosses. Manager Tom Watson kept faith with Bartrop and he retained his place in the team for the following match. This would be a visit to Bolton Wanderers on Christmas Day 1914. By now, the team and supporters were desperate for a positive result. Liverpool had gone seven games without a win and the club was sliding down the First Division table. The finger of blame was being pointed at the forwards, with one reporter even delivering a tongue-in-cheek reminder to manager Tom Watson and his team that shots only count when the ball actually finds the net: 'Goals count "for" and sins of omission "against". One inner is worth more than any number of outers. Have that framed T.W. and hung right on the door of the dressing room'.[9]

Christmas was ushered in by a severe cold spell, and several sporting events in the north of England were cancelled because of the conditions – sometimes the teams turned up and simply refused to play. Bolton did not escape the freeze and the surface of their pitch was slippery and frozen. Even so, the match against Liverpool went ahead as planned, and fifteen thousand spectators braved the icy winds. It was a scrappy game, with the treacherous conditions affecting the quality of the football. Bartrop again contributed well, outpacing the Bolton defenders on several occasions, providing some promising crosses, and hitting the side netting with a fierce shot. A single goal from Billy Lacey gave Liverpool the win, and offered their supporters relief from the team's miserable run of form. It did not, however, secure Bartrop a team place. The following day Sheldon replaced Bartrop for the Boxing Day fixture, a home game against Manchester United. Nowadays, having two games on consecutive days would give any manager an excuse to rest players, but it was not common policy in that era. With the FA insisting that each team must field its strongest team, ten of the players who had travelled to Bolton on Christmas Day also faced Manchester United on the 26th. Only Wilfred Bartrop was dropped.

Liverpool's form during the rest of the season remained erratic, but the club ultimately settled in a safe mid-table position. On Good Friday 1915, Liverpool travelled to Old Trafford to face Manchester United. This was to prove one of the most bizarre, and infamous, football matches ever to take place. The referee, John Sharpe, who had officiated in fussy fashion in Bartrop's debut against Oldham, described it as 'the most extraordinary match he had ever officiated in'.[10] United had been a force to be reckoned with over the previous few years, having won the First Division Championship in 1908 and 1911, plus the FA Cup in 1909. In 1915, however, they were having a dreadful season, and were close to the foot of the table. As one reporter wrote before the game: 'The position of Manchester United is now a desperate one, and it would need success in their three Easter engagements at Old Trafford – against Liverpool, Newcastle and Bradford (Park Avenue) – to take them out of the danger zone'.[11]

United's poor form in the league was despite the fact that they still had several of their stars, including Billy Meredith – a prolific striker in his youth. Meredith had spearheaded the campaign to increase the players' maximum wage in 1908; more contentiously, he had also been involved in an attempted match-fixing episode in 1905. While playing for Manchester City, he had offered the captain of Aston Villa £10 to throw a match.

On that rainy afternoon, 2 April 1915, fifteen thousand people stood on the terraces of Old Trafford to watch Manchester United play Liverpool. They were not impressed with what they witnessed. The Manchester United manager left before the final whistle, even though his team was winning. Shouts of 'Play up you rotters!'[12] came from the bored crowd. The reporter from the *Sporting Chronicle* called it 'The most uninteresting game ever seen on the ground'.[13] That comment, however, concealed the truth. It may not have been an exciting contest, but it was certainly interesting for other reasons. In the first half, Manchester United peppered the Liverpool goal with shots, and for forty minutes the scores were kept level primarily by the heroics of goalkeeper Elisha Scott. Five minutes before half-time, United striker George Anderson received the ball from the right and drove it into the Liverpool net, to the delight of the home supporters. Strangely, however, Liverpool had offered little attacking threat throughout the first half and seemed content to pass the ball around. The second half then started in a most peculiar way. Manchester United were awarded a penalty just a few minutes after the re-start, but Patrick O'Connell's[14] shot went 'ridiculously wide'.[15] The Liverpool team continued to provide little threat, and midway through the half Anderson added a second goal for United. After this, both teams seemed content to leave things at that, and 'the play in the concluding stages was too poor to describe'.[16] And so the match petered out at a 2–0 win to the home team, with one goal in each half.

This could easily have been put down to an off-day for Liverpool; after all they had been unpredictable throughout the season. However, a remarkable episode in the second half might have made any spectator suspicious. Liverpool's star marksman, Fred Pagnam broke through the United defence and his stinging shot hit the bar. He was then berated by his own players, seemingly angry that he should have done something so foolish. Did they really not want to see a Liverpool goal? A few weeks later it transpired that local bookmakers had received an unprecedentedly high number of bets on a 2–0 win to United at 7/1 odds. A Football League enquiry was launched immediately.

Many months later, the truth emerged. Jackie Sheldon, the former Manchester United player, and now Liverpool outside right, admitted to being the ringleader of the plan to fix the match, with the pre-arranged score of 2–0, with a goal in each half. Consistent with the brazen nature of the scheme, the planning by Sheldon and several United players actually took place in the Dog and Partridge – a well-known pub just across the road from the Old Trafford ground, hardly a place for clandestine plotting! Along with Sheldon, three other Liverpool players were implicated (Bob Pursell, Tom Miller and Tom Fairfoul), as were three Manchester United players (Enoch 'Knocker' West and two men not playing in the match, Sandy Turnbell and Arthur Whalley). Not all those named admitted involvement, but each received a life ban from playing football or even from entering a football ground. The other players were exonerated. Fred Pagnam, who had hit the United bar during the match, was one of the players who – despite knowing of the plan – stuck firmly to his principles, and tried throughout to win the match for Liverpool. At a hearing that took place before the High Court of Justice King's Bench Division, in 1917, Pagnam confirmed that he had 'threatened to bang one in', to which Sheldon replied that if he did 'he had bloody well finished in Liverpool'.[17] The former Barnsley player Phil Bratley had also played in the match but was not implicated. Wilfred Bartrop was absent – his position having been filled by the ring leader Sheldon.

Jackie Sheldon

In the months following the Old Trafford match, before the Football League commission had reported, Sheldon continued to play for Liverpool. In the tail end of that season, Bartrop displaced Sheldon for just one match, a 2–1 win at home over Bradford on 17 April 1915. So, with the exception of three appearances, Wilfred Bartrop had been kept out of the Liverpool team by a brilliant but flawed player. When Sheldon, his rival for the number seven position, received a life ban from football, the path should then have been open for Bartrop to take his place in the team for the 1915/16 season. But instead his way was now blocked by a far greater problem: the Great War.

## Chapter 9

# Football and war

This is no time for football. This nation, this Empire, has got to occupy itself with more serious business. The young men who play football and the young men who look on have better work to do. The trumpet calls them, their country calls them, the heroes in the trenches call them. They are summoned to leave their sport, and to take part in the great game. That game is war, for life or death.[1]

This was the rallying cry of the *Evening News* in September 1914, when announcing that it would no longer publish its Saturday football edition. Not only was it 'no time for football', it was also 'no time for football editions'. It was a mood shared by many people up and down the country. One correspondent to *The Times*, an academic from London by the name of A.F. Pollard, went even further, saying that 'every spectator who pays his gate money is contributing so much to a German victory'.[2] Pollard's view may have been extreme, but the general feeling was that some of the country's fittest men – the professional footballers – were being given a ready excuse not to enlist; and if they were not enlisting why should anyone else bother? The country's most celebrated cricketer, W.G. Grace, echoed the sentiments, and argued that the county cricket season should also be stopped: 'The fighting on the Continent is very severe and will probably be prolonged. I think the time has arrived when the county cricket season should be closed, for it is not fitting at a time like the present that able-bodied men should play day after day, and pleasure-seekers look on'.[3]

It was hard to disagree, but there was a counter-argument. Winning the war did not just involve fighting in the trenches, but also working in munitions factories, mining for coal and manning the country's essential services. The key workers on the home front, reading newspaper reports of the horrors occurring in Europe, also had to keep their morale high. Sport was a temporary escape from reality, without which the seriousness of life could become unbearable. Furthermore, so the Football Association and the clubs argued, football grounds could act as recruitment drives, where a rallying cry could be aimed at what was essentially a captive audience of (mainly) young men. There were actually relatively few professional football players, so perhaps the problem had been exaggerated. In September 1914, there were only some two thousand in Britain, and around two-thirds of these were married and not generally expected to enlist in these early days of the war.[4] As a consequence, there were not many more than several hundred able-bodied single men earning a living from playing football, instead of serving in the forces. By April 1915, one hundred and twenty-two of these had enlisted.[5] There was also another relevant point that the clubs emphasised several times. The professional players were under contract, and if football were prohibited, the clubs would be legally bound to continue paying their salaries. Unless an Act of Parliament intervened, the clubs simply could not afford to stop playing matches.

Accordingly, the Football Association and Football League continued as nearly normal as possible. Unlike their colleagues in Amateur Football, competition was not suspended, and a full programme of league and cup matches was completed in the 1914/15 season.[6] Some disruption did occur, however, because many players volunteered for the forces, the size of crowds dropped, and transfers between clubs effectively ceased. The manager of Liverpool Football Club, Tom Watson, demonstrated his support for the war effort, by encouraging two of his Directors and many shareholders to enlist and persuading the players to donate 12.5 percent of their wages to the armed forces. Many of the top-flight clubs introduced military drill training alongside regular training for their players, and several installed rifle ranges for daily practice. The FA also asked clubs to place their pitches and facilities at the disposal of the War Office on non-match days, for military training or other purposes. In certain cases, groups of professional footballers even formed their own army units, the 17th and 23rd Battalions of the Middlesex Regiment being the most famous. Large numbers of footballers and other sportsmen enlisted into these, and they became widely known as the First and Second 'Football Battalions'. Players from the Second Division side Clapton Orient were the first and keenest to join up, but both battalions drew recruits from many other clubs. Nor were they restricted to players either, with friends and supporters also being encouraged to enlist. One poster displayed at a London football ground appealed to the loyalty of the supporters in this way:

Do you want to be a
Chelsea Die-Hard?
If so
Join the 17th Battalion
Middlesex Regiment
'The Old Die-Hards'
And follow the lead given
by your favourite Football Players [7]

Despite the continuation of professional football, Wilfred Bartrop did not play a major part in Liverpool Football Club's league campaign for 1914/15. As already recounted, he was picked only three times for the first team. Nor did he feature in Liverpool's brief run in the FA Cup that season, which must have been a major disappointment considering his record in the competition. As a second-choice player, however, Bartrop was kept active with a busy schedule of Reserve Team league games and regional cups. These were decidedly less glamorous, but they did give him another cup winner's medal.

Wilfred Bartrop played twenty-eight games for the Liverpool Reserve Team in the Central League in 1914/15, and scored six goals.[8] He was appointed first choice penalty taker for the Reserves, and some of his more important goals came from the penalty spot. One occasion was on Good Friday 1915, when the First Team was away at Old Trafford for the notorious, and corrupt, match against Manchester United. On that same rainy afternoon, Bartrop was in the Liverpool Reserve team that played Stockport County Reserves at Anfield. Bartrop's telling contribution came in the final seconds of the game, when his penalty salvaged a 2–2 draw.[9] The very next day, his accuracy from the spot was tested again, when Anfield hosted Bartrop's former club Barnsley, albeit their Reserves. This was a more entertaining match, and press reports singled out Bartrop for praise. He almost scored in the first minute, led most of the attacks, and was 'master on his wing'.[10] Bartrop's penalty in the second half gave Liverpool the lead, which they extended to win 3–1. The match was unusual, even confusing, because the teams changed colours at half time, with Liverpool wearing red for the first half, and Barnsley in red for the second!

More exciting than Reserve Team leagues, for both players and spectators, were the local cup competitions. Some of these, such as the Liverpool Senior Cup, still run today and offer a fascinating opportunity for local amateur teams to compete against the big names. These days, clubs like Liverpool and Everton usually field their youth teams, while the non-league sides pick their first teams. In Bartrop's day, before the era of youth sides and academies, a mixture of Reserve and First Team players would compete on behalf of Liverpool FC. Wilfred Bartrop played for Liverpool in the Senior Cup competition in 1914/15, and scored in a 5–0 semi-final win over South Liverpool on 28 October 1914. This sent Liverpool through to the Final against Tranmere Rovers on 25 November. The match, held at Goodison Park, ended 1–1 in front of barely a thousand spectators. Because of wartime disruption, the replay did not take place until many months later, but strangely it was staged at Liverpool's home ground rather than another neutral venue. In this second match, on 10 April 1915, the two teams were again evenly matched and produced a hard fought and physical game. The two teams also knew each other well; in fact the goalkeepers appearing for Liverpool and Tranmere were two brothers. It was only a dubious penalty award in the first half that ultimately settled the match. Tranmere Rover's Ralph Holden was judged to have elbowed Fred Pagnam, and Bartrop stepped up to fire home the resulting penalty, the cup winning goal, in front of twelve thousand spectators.[11]

It was only a minor medal, and of mere local concern compared to the national attention given to the very continuance of football during the war. Two weeks after the Liverpool Senior Cup Final, on Saturday 24 April 1915, it was decreed that professional football would cease for the remainder of the war. On that day, the last of the First and Second Division league matches were played, Liverpool (without Bartrop) beat Oldham 2–0, and Barnsley beat Leeds City 2–0. But most interest was cast in the direction of Old Trafford, where the 1915 FA Cup Final was played. Almost fifty thousand spectators watched the favourites Sheffield United beat Chelsea 3–0, to lift the trophy for a third time.

This match at Old Trafford will always be remembered as the 'Khaki Cup Final', on account of the large numbers of servicemen amongst the crowd, either on leave from military training or already returned home from the war with injuries. The nature of the crowd served as a graphic reminder of the incongruousness of continuing with professional football while war raged in Europe. By now, the Football Association had bowed to public pressure. On the evening before the Cup Final, the FA adopted a resolution to suspend professional football for the remainder of the war. There was some debate as to what should happen to players; a decision was made later that the clubs would retain their registrations but not pay the players. Players were forbidden from seeking new contracts at other clubs, and so the income to clubs from future transfer fees was also safe-guarded. For the players, this was the worst possible outcome. Now unemployed, they were forced either to seek work outside football or to enlist in the army.

For Wilfred Bartrop, and other members of Liverpool Football Club, this was a time of great uncertainty. Wilfred's younger brother Percy enlisted in the Lincolnshire Regiment and was later wounded fighting in the Balkans, while an uncle, William Bartrop, was one of the very first men to join the famous Accrington Pals (part of the East Lancashire Regiment) on 14 September 1914. Wilfred, however, decided not to volunteer at this stage but to support the war effort in other ways. He returned to Nottinghamshire and sought work back at Manton Colliery.

Football remained a small part of Bartrop's life. Although professional football had ceased, a number of local leagues had been sanctioned, on condition that players were not paid and that matches took place only on Saturdays. Furthermore, any former professional was allowed to play for whichever team was closest to his home or place of work. Not all records have survived, but it is known that Wilfred Bartrop made an appearance for Notts County on 9 September 1916. Ironically, the opponents that day were Barnsley, the club with which he had spent the most successful and happiest times of his career. It seems probable he had offered his services to Notts County on this occasion simply because the visiting team was Barnsley, thereby giving him a chance to catch up with former team mates and friends. The match was remarkable in that, despite being an 'amateur' wartime game, it featured an England international and at least three FA Cup winners! The England star was defender Jesse Pennington, the West Bromwich Albion captain who had played against Bartrop in the 1912 Cup Final, and who now lined up alongside him for Notts County. The Barnsley team included two of the 1912 medal winners – Phil Bratley who had signed for Liverpool at the same time as Wilfred Bartrop, and Harry Tufnell who had scored the cup-winning goal in 1912. Despite the array of talent on show, only two thousand, five hundred people turned up at Meadow Lane to watch the match. Those who came saw the home team take the lead after just three minutes, when Bratley made an uncharacteristic error, his weak back pass being pounced on by Notts County striker G.H. Walker. Barnsley equalized midway through the first half through Kaye, and after that it was only the heroics of Albert Iremonger in the Notts County goal that ensured the scores stayed level. Wilfred Bartrop had a quiet game, with few of his trademark crosses from the right wing causing problems to the Barnsley defence.[12]

While war and football proceeded together uneasily in England, they became close partners on the battlegrounds of Europe. Football was popular amongst the troops as a means of recreation, and encouraged by officers, who appreciated its positive effect on team building. On the Western Front, where the front line was quite static for long periods of the war, the army could establish semi-permanent training areas far behind the danger areas. These were used not only for military training, but also for sporting competitions. There are many reports of Brigade and Battalion football tournaments, some of which were highly organised, with medals being presented. Moreover, although these matches were supposedly located beyond the range or accuracy of enemy shells, this could not be guaranteed. The diary of a Sergeant Major in the 3rd Infantry Middlesex Labour Company captured the situation well:

> March 21st – Quite an exciting day. Went to Dickebusch to see our corps football match. We won 2–1. Nearly got blown up at Remy siding. 3 shells burst behind the house I was passing. I was on horseback. Then got shelled at Anderdum and Dickebusch, they put one right in the football field.[13]

An even closer shave was recounted by Lance Sergeant Frederick Blakeman of the 7th Bedford Regiment in a letter home to a friend in 1916:

> The last time we were resting we managed to arrange a few games of football, my Company beating B by 3 goals to 2. During this match 'Fritz' got the range nicely, and planted several shells within 40yds of our pitch; no one was hurt but I have never seen a footer ground cleared so quickly. Eventually we returned and completed the game.[14]

The matter-of-fact way in which football and danger were mixed was quite typical of the time, but simply reflects how troops were becoming used to their precarious existence. Sport was always a salutary distraction, and highly valued for that, as Sergeant Blakeman further explained: 'You know a little bit of sport of this kind helps to keep up the boys' spirits, but our greatest regret now is that the ball you sent us is about played out, so should you know of anyone with an old football, no matter what condition it may be in, ask them to send it over here'.[15]

There were even a few occasions when a football appeared right in the trenches. The best-known example is associated with the 'Christmas truce' that took place in the first winter of the war, after fighting had been underway for just four months. As the first Christmas approached, soldiers in the German and Allied trenches took to singing carols, Silent Night or Stille Nacht being a favourite on both sides. These could be heard by enemy soldiers crouched in their own trenches, sometimes a mere hundred yards from each other, and they often drew applause. On occasions these exchanges led to shouts for temporary ceasefires, which were strongly discouraged by the commanding officers. It is now certain, however, that at several places along the Western front a temporary truce was agreed on or about Christmas Day 1914. Soldiers emerged from a rat-like existence in the miserable, frozen, holes and met their sworn enemies in the no-man's land running between the lines of trenches, primarily to retrieve and bury the bodies of their comrades, but also to swap stories, exchange gifts of tobacco or food and, occasionally, to play football.

There are several reports of these games, or impromptu kick-abouts as they really were, none of which paid much attention to rules of any kind. Most of the reports are second-hand, however, and details sketchy. One such example involved the Bedfordshire Regiment and German soldiers of the 19th Corps. On this occasion, a ball was produced from somewhere and the two groups of soldiers, who a matter of hours ago had been trying to kill each other, played until the ball became deflated when it was kicked onto an entanglement of barbed wire.

Another very well reported incident occurred in 1916, on the first day of the Battle of the Somme. But this was no kick-about during a ceasefire; it occurred in the heat of battle. On 1 July, after a massive bombardment of the German defences, half a million Allied troops awaited the signal to climb out of their trenches and advance across no-man's land to attack the enemy lines. Private L. S. Price of the 8th Royal Surrey Regiment recounted what happened next:

> As the gun-fire died away I saw an infantry man climb onto the parapet into no-man's land, beckoning others to follow. As he did he kicked off a football: a good kick, the ball rose and travelled well towards the German line. That seemed to be the signal to advance.[16]

The man at the centre of this action was Captain Wilfred 'Billie' Nevill of the 8th Battalion East Surrey Regiment, but this was no mindless act of bravado. It was a carefully planned event, designed to motivate the hundreds of young men about to face the most terrifying challenge of their lives. Nevill was fully aware that football was a bond between the infantry men; it could be used to spur his soldiers on, to reinforce their team spirit. In fact, Nevill had brought four footballs with him from England, and offered a prize to the first of his troops to dribble a ball over to the German front line. The prize was never claimed. As the East Surreys and their comrades stormed into no-man's land following their football, they expected to face little opposition from the shattered German lines. Instead, they met a barrage of machine-gun fire. Captain Nevill, along with thousands of others, died that day in the no-man's land of the Somme.

The Captain Nevill incident underlines how the game of football had already become a part of the nation's culture by the time of the First World War. Played by many, watched by more, it was a high point of weekly life for millions of men across Britain. Professional players were not yet millionaires or television idols, but they were well-known names and quite easily recognized, at least locally, by the man in the street. For young men at the front line, it must have been both strange and inspiring when the first professional footballers volunteered as regular soldiers, to fight side by side with those who had watched them from the terraces. One of the many professionals to join up was First Division player and FA Cup winner, Wilfred Bartrop.

## Chapter 10

# The Hindenberg Line

To understand Wilfred Bartrop's contribution to the war, it is necessary to go back to 1914 and the start of hostilities in Europe. In August 1914, the German First Army stormed across Belgium and into eastern France, with Paris in its sights. British and French forces were mobilized quickly and resisted the advance, albeit with huge loss of life. Ferocious battles ensued at Mons and Ypres, and the invading forces were ultimately checked in their tracks. By the end of 1914, an impasse had been reached. The British, French and Belgian armies were now 'dug in', forming a series of trenches running for several hundred miles, from the North Sea to Switzerland. The German forces, in a parallel line, faced the Allies across a no-man's land bristling with barbed wire and blasted with craters. A war of movement was now severely limited.

The Allied command discussed many options to break the deadlock. Sitting in a static defensive line along the Western Front was not one of them. Attack was seen as the best form of defence, certainly in the opinion of General Sir Douglas Haig, commander of the British forces. In his final dispatch, looking back on the course of the war, Haig eloquently explained his view:

> Closely connected with the question of casualties is that of the relative values of attack and defence. It is a view often expressed that the attack is more expensive than defence. This is only a half statement of the truth.

> Unquestionably, unsuccessful attack is generally more expensive

than defence, particularly if the attack is pressed home with courage and resolution. On the other hand, attack so pressed home, if skilfully conducted, is rarely unsuccessful, whereas, in its later stages especially, unsuccessful defence is far more costly than attack. Moreover, the object of all war is victory, and a purely defensive attitude can never bring about a successful decision, either in a battle or in a campaign. The idea that a war can be won by standing on the defensive and waiting for the enemy to attack is a dangerous fallacy, which owes its inception to the desire to evade the price of victory.[1]

Over the next three years, a series of battles broke out along the Western Front, as each side launched offensives and counter-offensives at the opposing lines, trying either to gain a few miles of ground or to capture strategic points in the landscape. Sometimes the goal was even more brutal, being simply an attempt to weaken or demoralise enemy forces by killing or injuring as many of their adversaries as possible. Such action always resulted in massive numbers of casualties on both sides. The Battle of the Somme remains the most awful of these horrific encounters along the Western Front. The battle began as an offensive strike by the British and French forces along the German line between Amiens and Peronne, about 80 miles north east of Paris. Its main aim was to weaken the German forces, and thereby relieve the pressure on the distant cathedral city of Verdun, which was under sustained artillery bombardment and infantry attack, and severely stretching the French forces. General Haig devised a 'shock and awe' strategy for the attack at the River Somme, involving an eight-day bombardment of the German defences using every artillery weapon at his disposal. Half a million men were then ready to pour through the gap that should have opened up in the German line.

On the 1 July 1916, the first wave of Allied infantry troops rose out of their trenches, going 'over the top' into no-man's land for a head-on attack. Row after row of men were mown down by machine gun fire as every wave of attack failed. It took two weeks of further shelling and infantry attack to achieve just a small gap in the German lines, but even this was quickly filled by reinforcements. The preliminary bombardment had clearly failed, leaving the infantry as easy targets. It later transpired that the German army had cleverly exploited their excellent defensive positions on their higher ground by digging into the chalk hillsides and reinforcing their shelters with concrete, greatly lessening the impact of the exploding shells. Nonetheless, the Allied forces persisted with the Somme offensive for a further five months, by which time around a million British, French and German men had lost their lives.

A few miles from the Somme, but far less well known, lies another harrowing battle site, Bourlon Wood. This dark and tangled woodland, close to the town of Cambrai, would later become a significant place for Wilfred Bartrop. Cambrai, thirty miles south of Lille, was recognised by all parties as a position of great strategic importance, and the area had been in German hands since the invasion of France in 1914. The occupied territory extended a few miles to the west of Cambrai, effectively being a northern continuation of the line held at the Somme. But this was no ordinary line of defence. The massive loss of life on the Somme in 1916 had forced von Hindenberg, Chief of Staff of the German Army, to re-think the whole strategy of the invading forces. Together with his Quartermaster General, Erich von Ludendorff, Hindenburg decided to build a massive system of defensive fortifications, designed to be impenetrable. The 'Siegfried Stellung' was up to five miles in width, comprising row after row of deep trenches, banks of extensive concrete bunkers and machine gun emplacements, miles of reinforced tunnels complete with electric lighting and, in front of every trench, a jungle of heavy-gauge barbed wire. The British called it the Hindenberg Line.

Having constructed the Hindenberg Line well within the safety of their own territory, the German army then retreated to a defensive position behind it, but not before destroying everything of possible use to the Allies. The scorched earth policy was taken to the extreme, and included blowing up bridges, setting dynamite traps in large buildings, and destruction of entire villages. It was against these fortifications, close to Cambrai, that Allied forces decided to attack in November 1917. The village of Bourlon and the neighbouring Bourlon Wood were key targets. If the Hindenberg Line could be smashed here, and if the Allies could regain control of Bourlon and Cambrai, then this would provide a perfect route for forces to stream into enemy territory. Allied forces would then be able to spread north and south, from behind the Hindenberg Line, circumventing the enormous defensive structures. Haig also had one trump card to play. Tanks. Hundreds of tanks. Large armoured vehicles had never before been used on such a scale in battle, but the terrain around Cambrai was flat and dry, at least compared to the quagmire of the Somme and Ypres, and seemed perfect for their deployment.

On 20 November 1917, at 6.20 a.m., the massive offensive began. Simultaneously, around a thousand Allied guns started shelling the Hindenberg Line, almost five hundred tanks rumbled forward, three hundred aircraft took off, and thousands of infantry stormed forward from the front line. Within a day, a six mile wide stretch of the Hindenberg Line had been smashed, and a four mile advance made into enemy territory. Bourlon had not yet been reached, but this was a remarkable success.[2,3]

Manton Colliery in the early part of the twentieth century

As the news reached Britain on 21 November the mood was one of jubilation. Church bells rang out in celebration right across the country, for the first time since the start of the war.[4] Wilfred Bartrop was one of millions of men still at home who heard that inspirational sound. Not everyone had been called upon to fight, because there were other jobs to be done in support of the war effort. For Bartrop, this meant coal. Manton Colliery, just outside Worksop, was one of the most productive coal mines in the midlands, and it was here that he had volunteered his services after the cessation of professional football in 1915. Coal mining has never been a glamorous occupation, and always dangerous; but equally it was an essential service, necessary to fuel the war. Coal was in great demand by the hundreds of factories churning out new tanks, weapons, aeroplanes and ammunition. That icy morning in Nottinghamshire, as optimism at last ran high on the home front, was the day before Wilfred Bartrop's 30th birthday.

With the first stages successfully achieved, the Allied forces moved to attack further key targets, as they advanced towards Bourlon and Cambrai. Of the many Divisions of the British Army involved in these actions, one is of special significance to this account. The 40th Division was a relatively new army unit, with comparatively little experience of the war in France. Within a few months Wilfred Bartrop would be fighting shoulder to shoulder with these new recruits. For now, the 40th Division had been given the difficult but crucial task of taking Bourlon village and Bourlon Wood. On 23 November 1917, the 121st Brigade of the 40th Division were to advance towards Bourlon village, while their comrades in the 119th Brigade were ordered to make an assault towards Bourlon Wood. This was no simple task. The wood dominates a ridge 150 feet above the surrounding land, and was bristling with German machine-gun emplacements.

At 10.30 a.m., the battle began. The 40th Divisional artillery fired a barrage of high explosives and shrapnel bombs towards the edge of the wood, which was followed quickly by a massive infantry charge. Around a dozen tanks followed, overtaking the infantry, who were now streaming across the open ground under fire. Large numbers of casualties were inevitable, but there were also many reports of astonishing bravery. One involved Lieutenant Colonel Kennedy of the Royal Welch Fusiliers, who charged up on horseback to command his troops, dismounted, and then lead his men on foot from the front, waving his cane ahead of them. He was dead within seconds. Or Sergeant Major Davies of the same battalion who, while under intense fire, knelt down in front of his troops to allow his shoulder to be used as a gun-rest. An enemy bullet struck him in the head.

Once the wood was reached, the Allied artillery could provide no more support, and it became a 'soldiers' battle' – a frenzied struggle of bayonets, rifles and machine guns, plus a stern test of endurance. Within the tangled and dense woodland, battalions of men frequently became split up or surrounded, and even occasionally fired on their own by mistake. All the while trees were crashing down, partly because of the 40th Division's own artillery bombardment of earlier, but also because by now a barrage of German shells was exploding around the Allied soldiers. One observer a few miles away noted in his diary with characteristic understatement: 'Bourlon Wood does not look at all pleasant – explosions in the wood and puff balls of shrapnel over it'.[5]

As the infantry of the 40th Division started to gain ground and occupy parts of the wood, the German artillery turned to another tactic – chemical warfare. Thousands of canisters bearing an ominous yellow cross were fired at the Allied positions in the woods. These contained the most dreaded of all the chemical weapons used in the war – blistering mustard gas. This was a horrific weapon that caused pain and panic more often than death, but it could be cruelly effective. Mustard gas is a volatile liquid which, when vaporized, attacks the eyes and respiratory system, or as a liquid causes burns and blisters. H.G. Wells explained:

> It spread unsuspected on the ground getting on to boots and clothing, being carried hither and thither. Slowly, as it vapourized, its presence was revealed. Discomfort came, a horrible suspicion, fear and then coughing and retching … It ate into the skin, inflamed the eyes; it turned the muscles into decaying tissue. It became a creeping disease of the body, enfeebling every function, choking, suffocating.[6]

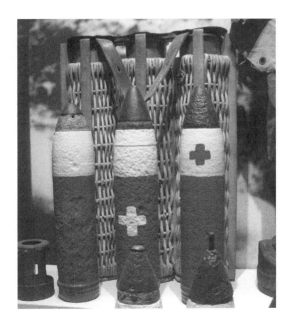

Yellow cross gas canister, centre

After two days and nights of ferocious fighting, the 40th Division captured Bourlon Wood; a day later parts of Bourlon village were also under Allied control. Victory came at a terrible price. More than three thousand men of the 40th Division had been killed, injured or captured in the three days of fighting. To recall the gallantry and heroism shown at Bourlon Wood, an acorn and two oak leaves were added to the divisional badge of the 40th Division. In later months, this was to be a badge worn by Wilfred Bartrop.

Chapter 11

# Bourlon Wood

One thousand shining white headstones stand in serried ranks, each facing the now celebrated Bourlon Wood. In the well-tended military cemetery outside the village of Annuex lie the bodies of over eight hundred British servicemen, many from the shattered 40th Division, and almost two hundred from Canada, New Zealand and Australia. Today, the hedgerows, the ploughed fields and the green woodland in the distance make for a peaceful scene. It is hard to visualise that back in the winter of 1917 this was hellish landscape. Close to the gate of the cemetery, in the sixth row of headstones, is the grave of Second Lieutenant F.G. Wheatcroft of the 13th East Surrey Regiment. This was a man well known to Wilfred Bartrop. On 30 March 1912, at Stamford Bridge, Freddie Wheatcroft had come within a whisker of depriving Bartrop of his FA Cup winner's medal.

Wheatcroft was one of the last truly amateur footballers competing at the highest level, including playing for the England Amateur Football Team He was a schoolteacher, but also played as inside forward – striker in today's terms – for Alfreton Town, Derby County, Swindon Town, Fulham and Reading Football Club. It was with Swindon Town that he enjoyed most success, when Swindon Town were in the Southern League and champions in 1910/11. On many occasions, they had matched or bettered their

Second Lieutenant
F.G. 'Freddie'
Wheatcroft

fully professional Football League colleagues when drawn against them in the FA Cup. In 1910 they had reached the semi-final of the Cup, then to lose to the eventual winners Newcastle United; in 1911 they made the quarter-finals, and in 1912 the semi-finals again. Few teams, professional, semi-professional or amateur, could claim such consistency. Freddie Wheatcroft had been a regular and important member of the side, although he was absent for Swindon Town's victory over Barnsley in the Dubonnet Cup played in Paris in the summer of 1910. Two years later, he encountered Wilfred Bartrop in the semi-final of the FA Cup. Although the match ended goalless, two of those who came closest to scoring were Wheatcroft and Bartrop. In the Barnsley goal, Jack Cooper produced a fingertip save to deny Wheatcroft the opening goal, while in the second half Bartrop hit the side netting with a fierce shot from a tight angle. The replay saw Barnsley advance to the Final, ultimately victorious, but it was a very close call. If Freddie Wheatcroft's shot had gone in, he and not Bartrop could have been the holder of a cup winner's medal.

Second Lieutenant Wheatcroft and the 13th East Surrey Regiment were part of the 40th Division that had captured Bourlon Wood and parts of Bourlon village in November 1917. On 26 November 1917, the order came to withdraw the 40th Division, so that the weary and depleted troops could be replaced with fresh men from the 62nd Division. Despite the early successes, which had set those church bells ringing in England, this was never going to be a simple withdrawal. The 13th East Surreys posed a particular problem. Wheatcroft, together with other officers and men, had advanced ahead of the rest of the Allied line and by 26 November they were in a very dangerous predicament. Ten tanks had been supposed to support their advance, but these never materialized. To make matters worse, the troops who, it was planned, would be providing covering fire, had been forced back by the enemy. As a consequence, the 13th East Surreys had become completely isolated from the rest of the Division, on the edge of Bourlon village. They sought shelter inside a deserted house, but with no support soon found themselves under intense machine-gun fire and artillery attack. The walls around them were gradually demolished as shell after shell hit its target. Several men escaped from the house into an improvised dug-out shelter in Bourlon Wood, but they had not reached safety. The withdrawal of the 40th Division went ahead as ordered; there was no rescue launched for the 13th East Surreys.[1] On 27 November 1917, Second Lieutenant F.G. Wheatcroft, footballer and teacher, died in action alongside so many of his troops.

Over the next few months that followed these ferocious battles, the tide turned against the Allies. The German army mounted a massive counter attack to retake Bourlon Wood and smash the defences beyond it. In fact, so successful was the German response that the Allies lost all the ground that had been gained in November, and they were pressed further and further back. Along most of the Western Front, the German army appeared to be gaining the ascendancy. The future of the war now hung in the balance.

In January 1918, Wilfred Bartrop joined up to fight. The early months of the year were filled by rigorous training at home in England, learning

Anneux Cemetery at the foot of Bourlon Wood

how to fight and how to deploy the vast array of field guns, howitzers and mortars for use in battle. The training was highly focussed, because Bartrop had opted not to become part of the infantry but to enlist in the Royal Field Artillery. Gunner Bartrop, serial number 252418, became specialised in the use of a particular weapon, the Trench Mortar. In June 1918, he was assigned to one of the Medium Trench Mortar Batteries within the 40th Division, the 'X/40' Battery. On 13 June 1918, he arrived in France.[2]

Following several disastrous battles in the early days of the war, the Allied and German armies had settled on a fairly standard routine for their offensive actions. First, the artillery, positioned behind the front line, would open fire with a barrage of explosives, in an attempt to destroy enemy guns, flatten barbed wire and prepare the ground for the infantry. Only then would the P.B.I. or Poor Bloody Infantry go 'over the top' and attack with rifles and bayonets. The infantry always bore the brunt of the casualties, as they were first in the line of enemy fire. Being in an Artillery Brigade was certainly a safer option, but it was no easy ride. After all, the enemy regularly aimed explosive shells at their positions, where artillery men would be standing surrounded by piles of live ammunition.

A bewildering diversity of artillery weapons was used by Allied forces, each gun designed for a different task. The mainstay of the Divisional Artillery was the 18-pound field gun, a giant rear-loaded cannon weighing over a ton and capable of firing shells at targets up to five miles away. These were the key weapons used in initial bombardment of enemy defences. But for close range work, for example against enemy machine guns or sniper posts, a more flexible and manoeuvrable weapon was needed. This was the domain of Gunner Bartrop and the Trench Mortars. Introduced by the Germans, and swiftly copied by the Allies, Trench Mortars were rather simple guns consisting of a long metal tube, like a section of drainpipe, closed at one end and with a firing mechanism inserted at the base. The charges were dropped down the barrel and then a high explosive bomb, shaped like half a dumbbell, would be inserted with the enlarged sphere sitting on the end. The men would rapidly then take cover as the bomb was fired in a looping arc, perhaps only a few hundred yards toward the enemy.

It was dangerous work, not only because of the occasional bomb that fired incorrectly, but because – as the name suggests – the Trench Mortars operated close up to the front line trenches. They were key targets for enemy attack.

Wilfred Bartrop arrived at Barly, 50 miles west of Cambrai, in June 1918. The artillery of the 40th Division, to which he had been assigned, was resting, training and generally preparing far behind the front line. The infantry of the 40th Division had been moved further north, to a supposedly quieter area near Lille, while the artillery had been left

An Allied Trench Mortar in action during the First World War

behind to support the 62nd Division and the Canadians, still holding the line west of Cambrai. A few weeks' training behind the front line was the usual means of gently orienting new recruits to life in the field – an introduction to the practicalities of war, and an exposure to the stream of casualties, but without being directly in the firing line. The official War Diary of Bartrop's Trench Mortar Battery gives a rather bland account of life at Barly, reporting training at the 4th Army Trench Mortar School, an inspection by Brigadier General C.E Palmer and, in an equally matter of fact way, reporting 'July 26th, X/40 T.M.B. HQ shelled by enemy'.[3] Even training was hazardous.

This was actually a signal to begin their offensive, and on 31 July 1918 the 40th Division artillery went into action. Over the next month, Bartrop and the Trench Mortar batteries moved forward in support of the advancing 52nd (Lowland) Division, overcoming German resistance on several occasions. On 22 August, preparations were made for an infantry attack on the Henin Trench system, originally in the hands of the Allies but now occupied by German troops. The Trench Mortar batteries were given the task of preparing the way, and twenty-nine rounds of ammunition were fired in an attempt to destroy enemy machine-gun posts and trench mortars before the infantry could advance. Twenty-nine rounds were quite insufficient to destroy any serious defensive system and it is clear that Captain Reid, the Division Trench Mortar Officer, had wished to be far more aggressive in his preparations. However, his heavy guns could not get close enough to the enemy targets, while his lighter and mobile Trench Mortars had simply run out of ammunition. In the normally dry and succinct War Diary, tersely logging every movement and interaction, he wrote an unusually angry entry for this day, venting his frustration:

> All T.M.'s now out of range. Mobile T.M.'s could have been taken forward in support of advance, or captured light T.M.'s could have been used, but transport for ammunition was not available. Mobile Trench Mortars are of no use unless ammunition is made mobile.[4]

The German armies were now being pressed right across the Western

Front, and here was no exception. In the two weeks from late September to the middle of October 1918, the Divisional Trench Mortar batteries supported the advancing 63$^{rd}$ Division in a very successful push that brought them right to the edge of Cambrai. They encountered dogged resistance and fighting at every village in their path – Anneux, Fontaine-Notre-Dame, Proville and Niergnes – but in each case the enemy was forced further into retreat. Inevitably, several of the gunners were killed in the process and at least two of the Trench Mortars put out of action by enemy fire. The village of Proville in particular proved to be very well defended by machine-gun emplacements, and it took five days of fighting to break through. Bartrop's X/40 Trench Mortars, together with the Y/40 Battery, fired almost a thousand rounds of shells at those emplacements to clear them before the infantry could advance, but in time the Germans were forced to retreat even from here. On 10 October 1918, the cathedral town of Cambrai was finally liberated.

Since their invasion in 1914, Cambrai had been the German army's most important base in the north. Its importance was due not just to its size and abundance of useful buildings and facilities, but also because of the many good roads and railway lines that ran from here into Germany, allowing efficient transport of troops, equipment, ammunition and supplies. For much of the war it had been considered so safe, and so well protected by the Hindenburg Line defence, that it had become the key base for training of German troops and planning of operations, and for battle-weary soldiers to rest and recover. For this, Cambrai had earned the nickname the 'Flanders sanatorium'. Now, in October 1918, it had been reached by the Allies, and Cambrai was returned to France. The town lay in ruins, however. More than six thousand houses had been destroyed, through a combination of artillery bombardment and deliberate sabotage by the retreating German troops. Rising above the burnt ashes stood the cathedral, which still today bears the scars of battle.

It had been a remarkably successful advance, but amid it occurred one of the most shocking events in the whole of Wilfred Bartrop's time on the Western Front. It happened in the middle of September 1918, when the Allied troops were still seven miles west of Cambrai. The first fortnight of September had been quiet in terms of front-line action, but

The remains of Cambrai, 1919

this time was not spent resting. Preparations were being laid for a major assault. The troops were close to the villages of Inchy and Moeuvres, on the west bank of the Canal du Nord. This is now a major waterway carrying huge commercial barges, but in 1918 it had recently been dug and was essentially a giant dry ditch. It was also a difficult line to cross, as German troops occupied trenches and gun emplacements at intervals along the far bank. Over two miles away, in the direction of Cambrai, rose the heights of Bourlon Wood where so many of the 40th Division had been killed in 1917, including the footballer Freddie Wheatcroft.

The Allied plan now was to advance in two directions. The British 63rd Division, supported by the artillery of the 40th Division, would move south of the wood, taking the villages along the Baupame to Cambrai road. Simultaneously, Canadian troops would sweep directly east, with the daunting task of retaking Bourlon Wood which the Germans had held since the battles of 1917. But first, something needed to be done to pave the way for the Canadian advance. The task that fell to the X/40 and Y/40 Trench Mortar batteries, including Gunner Bartrop, was to evict as many Germans as possible from Bourlon Wood. The wood was far too distant to be reached using Trench Mortars, but they did have another option. During the previous month, four German 77mm cannons had been captured − giant guns capable of firing shells at targets up to five miles away. Those first two weeks of September, therefore, were spent collecting enemy ammunition for use in the

View across Canal du Nord from Moeuvres, with Bourlon Wood
in the distance, 2006. The X/40 Trench Mortar Battery operated German
77mm canons from this position.

German guns, ready for firing at the distant Bourlon Wood. And the
principal ammunition found was not explosives, but large canisters
marked with that ominous yellow cross. It was, of course, the feared
blistering mustard gas.

On 11 September 1918, the four 77mm guns were swung around and
pointed back at their previous owners, now encamped in Bourlon
Wood. Every night for two whole weeks, those guns, manned by the
Trench Mortar personnel, blasted the distant woods with canisters of
mustard gas. In total, an astonishing three thousand rounds of Yellow
Cross Gas[5] were fired at the wood in one of the most ferocious
chemical warfare attacks made by British troops. There is no hint of
remorse in the War Diaries. This was seen simply as handy ammunition
suitable for the job at hand. It came from the enemy, and now it was
going back.

It was not the only time that Allied soldiers used chemical weapons in the First World War. Indeed there was to be another memorable episode just a month later, further north near the Belgian village of Werwick. There an Austrian-born Corporal in the German army wrote vividly of his experiences:

> We were subjected for several hours to a heavy bombardment with gas bombs, which continued throughout the night with more or less intensity. About midnight a number of us were put out of action, some for ever. Towards morning I also began to feel pain. It increased with every quarter of an hour; and about seven o'clock my eyes were scorching as I staggered back and delivered the last dispatch I was destined to carry in this war. A few hours later my eyes were like glowing coals and all was darkness around me.[6]

The writer's name was Adolf Hitler.

## Chapter 12

## The Advance to Victory

We shall never sheathe the sword, which we have not lightly drawn, until Belgium receives in full measure all and more than she has sacrificed, until France is adequately secured against the menace of aggression, until the rights of smaller nationalities of Europe are placed upon an unassailable foundation, and until the military might of Prussia is wholly and finally destroyed.[1]

This was the declaration made by the Prime Minister, Herbert Asquith, at the start of the war. Four years later, on 14 October 1918, *The Times* repeated his words in its leader as a rallying cry to the nation. The end of the war was in sight, but there was consternation about exactly how it would end. The German army was in retreat, at least over much of the Western Front, and government representatives were desperately trying to negotiate a ceasefire to protect their troops. The American President, Woodrow Wilson, together with the then Prime Minister Lloyd George and the French leader Clemenceau, firmly rejected the German proposals, however, and determined upon a full-scale surrender. Commentators in Britain were unanimous in their support for America's hard stance. On the front line, the killing continued.

After their success at Cambrai, the 40th Division artillery, including Wilfred Bartrop, were sent 40 miles north to join their own infantry at Armentieres, close to the city of Lille. They arrived on 18 October 1918, along with letters of praise and commendation. In reference to the X/40 Divisional Trench Mortar Battery, General Sir Charles Ferguson wrote:'The trench mortar personnel also did excellent work in manning the 77mm battery at Moeuvres and dosing Bourlon Wood with yellow cross gas, with the result that the German batteries were captured there in situ'.[2]

General Waldrop, in overall command of artillery for the British Third Army added:'It is hard to speak too highly of them and their work'.[3]

Bartrop and the other Trench Mortar personnel were able to rest and train at Armentieres for a full week, before moving twenty miles east to Lannoy, a village close to the border between France and Belgium, and just 10 miles behind the front line. Here another week was spent training and obtaining supplies, including four new Mobile Trench mortars; and by 6 November they were prepared to go into action again. The Battery had not faced the enemy for almost a month. Entries in the official War Diary reveal how they kept themselves in readiness to fight, although one entry written at Lannoy now reads alarmingly if taken literally: 'No targets to fire at. Only Belgian civilians'.[4]

On 6 November, the Divisional Trench Mortar Batteries moved forward the last few miles to join the infantry around the villages of Warcoing and Pecq in Belgium. Here, the advancing troops had met a major barrier to their progress, the River Escaut, known in Flemish as the Scheldt. This deep and powerful waterway would present a challenge at any time, but it was also heavily defended by the enemy. Although the weakened German armies were generally in retreat, there were places along the front line where they were not moving without a fight. The River Escaut was one such spot. Here machine-gun emplacements and bunkers protected the eastern bank, while artillery positions were close enough to fire shells across the river with accuracy. In the village of Herinnes, just half a mile east of the river, German troops were using the church tower as an observation post, so any attempt by the British to cross the river could be spotted. As a result, the German army knew the exact movements of the British 40th Division.

River Escaut, Warcoing, Belgium

Warcoing and Pecq lie just two miles apart on the west bank of the Escaut, directly opposite Herinnes. At the start of November, the German artillery had started to shell both villages heavily. Many civilians were still in their houses, and took refuge in cellars expecting the attacks to pass quickly. They didn't. After a week of bombardment, the 40ᵗʰ Division Field Ambulance was forced to evacuate many inhabitants, even 'going right up to Pecq to take out of their houses nervous old ladies whilst shelling was actually in progress'.[5]

Repelling the Germans from their well-defended positions was a serious challenge. The immediate goal was clear enough: troops would have to cross the swift-flowing River Escaut and storm Herinnes. In the last few days of October and the start of November, several attempts were made to send small groups of men across the river as advance patrols. This involved throwing a footbridge and trying quickly to storm the enemy, hoping to retain the element of surprise. Again and again the patrols came under machine-gun fire or Trench Mortar attack and were forced to retreat. Two patrols, however, succeeded in capturing enemy machine gun posts in broad daylight, and even returned with prisoners. There was also a remarkable incident that earned a medal for one of the officers. Captain T. Cowcher had seen an Allied plane shot down in aerial combat, and spotted that it had come to land on the east bank of the river. The pilot and observer crawled out alive but injured, and then slowly started to move in the direction of some nearby buildings. What they had not realised, but was only too clear to Captain Cowcher, was that inside the buildings were German troops. The officer dived into the Escaut and swam across to the enemy-held east bank. There he caught up with the two injured airmen, warned them of the hidden danger in the buildings, and swam back across the river with both men, under a hail of bullets. He was recommended for the Victoria Cross, for 'valour in the face of the enemy' but, to the surprise of his troops, his bravery was rewarded with the Military Cross for 'gallantry in the field'.[6]

The patrols had mostly failed, but they had served to show the determination of the German forces east of the Escaut. Even so, the British forces were almost certainly superior in number, and so a large-scale assault would most likely be successful. The commanding officers decided that the Escaut would be crossed in a major attack, aiming to overwhelm the enemy. The date set for the 'full dress forcing' of the river was 7 November 1918.[7] As it happened, the end of war was just four days away, but this could not be known to those on the front-line. At the time, the only objective was to continue to put pressure on the retreating armies, to drive them across Belgium and possibly right into Germany.

Before the infantry could advance, the plan was for the artillery to lessen the threat from enemy machine guns and mortar emplacements. Gunner Bartrop was in action again. On 6 November, he and the other members of the Battery manned their Trench Mortars at Warcoing, firing shells at enemy machine-gun emplacements just across the river, preparing the ground for the advance. The process continued on the following day. It was dangerous work, of course, because whenever a gun was fired it drew attention to its own position. One of the official

War Diaries reports how passive the enemy was on the 4 November, before a sudden and ferocious enemy bombardment took place for three days on 5, 6 and 7 November, aimed directly at the village of Warcoing. November 4th had been quiet enough for the officer to write about how many in the battalion were suffering from colds and influenza, but on the following days the focus was only on the fighting.[8] Just how intense the shelling was is indicated by the large number of Allied troops who were rapidly withdrawn out of Warcoing, back to safer positions. By contrast, Bartrop and the other gunners were left in place.

On 7 November 1918, Wilfred Bartrop and a fellow gunner came under enemy fire while moving one of their artillery guns into position. Shells were exploding around them as the German guns had found their range. Suddenly, one shell landed right next to Bartrop and exploded. The splinters of shrapnel hit him across the legs and chest. 'I am hit in the leg', he yelled, and then instantly collapsed.[9] Those were his last words. Charles Henry Wilfred Bartrop, professional footballer and FA Cup winner, died in action on 7 November 1918.

This was to prove to be the very last day of action seen by the 40th Division. The enemy shelling fell silent on 8 November; when patrols were sent across the river to investigate, they found that the German armies had retreated. Three days later, the headquarters of the 40th Division received the now famous telegram from GHQ whose message was fast spreading across the Western Front. The war had ended.

Following message from GHQ begins. Hostilities will cease 11.00 November 11th. Troops will stand fast on line reached at that hour. Defence precautions will be maintained. There will be no intercourse of any description with enemy until receipt of instructions from GHQ. Further instructions follow. Ends.

Gunner Wilfred Bartrop's grave, Warcoing

# Epilogue

On 7 November 1918, Wilfred Bartrop became one more statistic in a war that claimed the lives of millions. He was among the last men to die in the Great War. At 11 a.m. on 11 November 1918 the guns finally fell silent over the Western Front. In this biography I have traced Wilfred Bartrop's life through success and disappointment, through triumph and tragedy. Properly his story ends here, on the battlefields of Europe. But there are still a few loose ends to tie up. In particular, it is fitting to consider what happened to the 40th Division and to Bourlon Wood, to revisit the scandal at Liverpool Football Club, and to notice the fate of Barnsley's other cup winners, the future of Worksop Town Football Club and the lives of Wilfred's family. But first, the man himself.

Many of those who died in the Great War have no known resting place, and their names are inscribed on permanent memorials throughout Europe. Wilfred Bartrop's body was recovered from the battlefield and he is buried in the village of Warcoing, Belgium, close to where he fell. This is a small churchyard in a quiet agricultural community, quite unlike the vast military cemeteries found elsewhere in Flanders. Most of the graves here are of local people from the village of Warcoing, but alongside them are the graves of four Allied servicemen. None of the other three soldiers whose remains lie here fought with Bartrop, but all died in this area in those last few weeks during the Advance to Victory. Each was a young serviceman, killed just before the end of hostilities. Private H. Stanton from Birmingham, and serving in the 16th Battalion Manchester Regiment, was killed in action on 22 October 1918. He was 19 years old. Private D.T. Pilcher from Folkestone, serving with the 31st Battalion Machine Gun Corps, died a day earlier. He too was 19. Second Lieutenant Harold Perveval Nixon from Belfast, of the 6th Battalion Wiltshire Regiment, was killed on 26 October 1918. He was 22. Wilfred Bartrop, buried next to them, was 30.

We left the 40th Division attempting to cross the River Escaut in Belgium following fierce resistance from German machine guns and artillery. As the German armies withdrew, the infantry of the Division bridged the river successfully, and by the 9 November 1918 they had re-captured the village of Herinnes. The main troops advanced another seven miles to beyond the village of Clipet, while patrols pushed on further to reach the town of Velaines. During this advance, the Divisional Trench Mortar Batteries stayed at Warcoing and Pecq. On 10 November, Allied troops from the north and south were converging towards the same point, and so the 40th Division was ordered to withdraw. The following morning GHQ's telegram was received, announcing the ceasefire.

Warcoing cemetery with graves of Bartrop and
three other Allied servicemen

The other scene of action experienced by Wilfred Bartrop had been the advance to Cambrai in eastern France, and along the way the recapture of Bourlon Wood. Today, Bourlon Wood still stands prominently above the surrounding landscape, and it is not hard to see why it was such an important site strategically. From its heights are commanding views of the main Bapaume to Cambrai road to the south, the Canal du Nord to the east, and the village of Bourlon to the north. All these targets could be fired upon from the wood, peppered with shells, or simply observed. At the edge of the wood there is a large clearing, where a great stone memorial now stands. Reached up a grand series of terraces cut into the hillside, and flanked by an avenue of lime trees, this memorial commemorates the men of the Canadian Corps who fought for Bourlon Wood in September 1918, following the initial bombardment from Bartrop and the 40th Division artillery. The memorial bears the same inscription in French and in English: 'The Canadian Corps on 27th Sep. 1918 forced the Canal du Nord and captured this hill. They took Cambrai, Denain, Valenciennes & Mons; then marched to the Rhine with the victorious Allies'.

At the end of the Great War, few locals would enter Bourlon Wood. Many thousands of men had died in within its dark interior and, although many were recovered for burial nearby, it is certain that some bodies still lie here. The wood today still has a maze of deep, rutted tracks – the same tracks along which the tanks of the 40th Division attempted to advance in November 1917. Alongside the paths lie numerous pits and hollows, tangled with brambles and thick with mud. Here men sheltered and fought, but they are best not explored today. Even now, some 90 years later, there are unexploded shells and canisters of chemical weapons buried in the ground and hidden amongst the tangled tree roots, which are still capable of detonating. Only a few years ago a tractor extracting timber went over an unexploded German shell, releasing a cloud of poisonous phosgene gas.

Liverpool Football Club was the last club that Bartrop played for, in the controversial 1914/15 season. The match-fixing inquiry reported in December 1915, and resulted in four Liverpool players receiving life bans from football: Jackie Sheldon, Bob Pursell, Tom Miller and Tom

Fairfoul, plus Manchester United's 'Knocker' West, Sandy Turnbell and Arthur Whalley. A few weeks later, the Football League made a further announcement on the matter. Remarkably, it was decided that although the game at Old Trafford had been fixed, the result would still stand. This meant that Manchester United avoided relegation by one point. Chelsea were saved from relegation only by expansion of the First Division in 1919. As for Wilfred Bartrop, he must have assumed that because his rival for the number seven position was now banned for life, he would be back at Liverpool playing First Division football after the end of hostilities. And with the German armies in retreat throughout October 1918, he and everyone else knew the end of the war was close. His return to Liverpool FC and the resumption of his professional career must have seemed imminent. But there is still one final ironic twist to the story. Even had Wilfred Bartrop survived the war, his path back to Liverpool's first team would have been blocked. After the Armistice, Sheldon and the other three Liverpool players implicated in the scandal had their bans lifted by the FA in recognition of their war service. Sheldon returned to football and continued to play for Liverpool until 1921, when a broken leg ended his career.

As for Barnsley, there were 12 players who had shared FA Cup glory in 1912, including Bert Leavey who missed the semi-final and final because of injury. Of the 12, only Wilfred Bartrop was killed in the First World War. The hostilities, however, claimed the lives of many footballers from other clubs. Two of those were members of the FA Cup winning team from the previous year. Bob Torrance and Jimmy Speirs had played for Bradford City in the 1911 Cup Final, with Speirs scoring the winning goal. Speirs also scored in the 1912 semi-final against Bartrop's Barnsley. Jimmy Speirs became a Seargent in the Queen's Own Cameron Highlanders, was awarded the Military Medal, and died in the horrific Third Battle of Ypres at Passchendaele in the summer of 1917. His team mate Bob Torrance was, like Wilfred Bartrop, a gunner in the Royal Field Artillery; Torrance was killed in April 1918. The longest surviving member of the Barnsley cup-winning team was Jimmy Moore, who was only 20 years old at the time of the Cup Final. For many years he was landlord of a pub in Barnsley, The Victoria, and was well known to locals and football supporters. Speaking to the *Daily*

*Express* in 1970, Moore gave his views on how football had changed: 'We were not pampered like they are now. I got a basic wage of £2 a week and another 15s if I got into the first team... The big treat was when manager Arthur Fairclough gave us £1 each so that we could but a smart new shirt apiece'. And as for performances on the pitch, he added 'I think we could show the current finalists a thing or two'.[1] Jimmy Moore died in December 1972 aged 81.

Barnsley's FA Cup triumph of 1912 hit the news again in 2008. Newspaper articles featured pictures of Bartrop and his teammates, and stories of the final were recounted once more. The reason for the interest was another incredible FA Cup run, this time seeing Barnsley progress to the semi-finals. This was a tremendous achievement for a team from the second tier of English football, but even more remarkable for the fact that Barnsley had defeated both Liverpool and Chelsea in the process. There was even a prospect of a repeat of the 1912 final, because West Bromwich Albion had reached the other semi-final. Ultimately, it was not to be, as Cardiff City narrowly defeated Barnsley 1–0, while Portsmouth, the only Premiership team left in the competition, beat West Bromwich Albion by the same score. In the midst of this feverish excitement, a rare cup winner's medal from one of the 1912 heroes came up for auction. On 27 February 2008, Wilfred Bartrop's FA Cup winner's medal went under the hammer at Bonhams, sold by an anonymous vendor. The experts had anticipated that the medal, just 3cm in diameter, would sell for between four and six thousand pounds. They were astounded by what happened. An expectant hush fell across the auction room in Chester as lot number 342 was reached, and bidding took off at a furious rate. Within seconds, the estimated price had been breached, yet bidding continued apace. The 15 carat gold medal, in superb condition, was finally sold for £14,400, more than double the estimated price.

Before Barnsley FC spotted his talents, Bartrop played for Worksop Town. The club is still in existence today, although it has had mixed fortunes over the years. In Bartrop's time, the club played in the Midland League, and this remained their level for many years. After several promotions and relegations, and a move to a new ground, the club is now thriving. In 2004, Worksop became one of the founding members of the Conference North – just five Divisions below the English Premiership. The year 2007 then saw the club drop down a further tier of the football pyramid. There have been several links to Barnsley FC in recent years, echoing Wilfred's move between the clubs back in 1909; for example, recent Worksop Town manager Ronnie Glavin was a former Barnsley player. I first watched Worksop Town play in a pre-season friendly against local non-league side AFC Emley in July 2006. Perhaps a future FA Cup winner was amongst them. On that evening, Worksop Town beat Emley by an emphatic six goals to one.

Finally, what of Wilfred Bartrop's family? At the end of the war, Ruby received the letter that every wife or mother dreaded. Captain J.E. Beningfield wrote: 'I sincerely regret to have to inform you that your husband, who served in my battery, was killed on the 7$^{th}$ November'.[2] After a short description of his last moments, the officer's letter concludes with, 'Please accept my deepest sympathy in your great loss. Gunner Bartrop was a sterling fellow and did very good work with me'. The text of the telegram was published in the local newspaper for all to see. Ruby later remarried and moved to the Lincolnshire coast. Many years later, disaster was to hit her life again when massive storms in 1953 caused devastating floods along the east coast of England. Ruby's home was among those destroyed. She died a few months later, aged 63.

Ruby and Wilfred had been married for six years when he was sent into action in France, but unusually they had no children. Although there are no direct descendents of Wilfred Bartrop, there are many other surviving relatives. Wilfred's father and grandfather, both called Benjamin Bartrop, were each very prolific, or rather their wives were. As a consequence, the Bartrop family is large, particularly around the Worksop area. Branches of the family have now spread out far and wide, and can be found from Nottingham to New Zealand. I am one of those many distant relatives. Wilfred's grandfather Benjamin Bartrop was also my great-great-grandfather.

# References

## Chapter 1
## The Bartrops of Worksop

1.  *Domesday Explorer* v. 1.0. Professional edition. Phillimore and Co. Ltd, 2000.
2.  BBC1 *Match of the Day*, 19 August 1995, referring to Manchester United's young team. The 'kids' went on to win the double of the FA Cup and Premier League in 1995/96.
3.  *Worksop Guardian*, 11 February 1910.
4.  M.J. Jackson. 1992. *Victorian Worksop*. p. 124.
5.  Ibid. pp. 53, 125.
6.  Worksop in 1850, *Worksop Guardian*, 28 November 1902.
7.  Ibid.
8.  M.J. Jackson. 1992. *Victorian Worksop*. p. 53.
9.  *Worksop Guardian*, 11 February 1910.
10. Bob Guirdham, personal communication.
11. *Worksop Guardian*, 9 May 1879.
12. Obituary, *Worksop Guardian*, 17 August 1951.
13. June Guirdham, personal communication.
14. Dawn Storer, personal communication.
15. Written and composed by Harry Hemsley; www.ovaltine.co.uk
16. Dawn Storer, personal communication.

## Chapter 2
## Shamrocks and Pensioners

1.  *Worksop Guardian*, 17 January 1908.
2.  Attendance figures for this match vary greatly between reports.

Figure quoted here from *Worksop Guardian*, 17 January 1908.

3. *Worksop Guardian*, 17 January 1908.
4. Ibid.
5. Football Gossip by Wide-Awake, *Worksop Guardian*, 6 March 1908.
6. Ibid, 13 March 1908.
7. Ibid.
8. Ibid.
9. Ibid, 20 March 1908.
10. Ibid, 24 April 1908.
11. *Doncaster Gazette* quoted in *Worksop Guardian*, 1 May 1908.
12. Football Jottings by Wide-Awake, *Worksop Guardian*, 24 April 1908.
13. Football Gossip by Wide-Awake, *Worksop Guardian*, 11 September 1908.
14. Ibid.
15. Ibid, 30 April 1909.
16. *Worksop Guardian*, 25 June 1909.

## Chapter 3
## Battling Barnsley

1. From a Correspondent, *The Times*, 22 April 1911.
2. *The Sporting Chronicle*, 22 April 1912.
3. *Barnsley Chronicle*, 12 March 1910.
4. Ibid.
5. *Yorkshire Telegraph and Star*, quoted in *Barnsley Chronicle*, 12 March 1910.
6. 'Tam' writing in *Morning Leader*, quoted in *Barnsley Chronicle*, 12 March 1910.
7. Ibid.
8. Postcard produced by Irving of Barnsley, 1910.
9. *The Times*, 1 April 1910.
10. *Sheffield Daily Telegraph*, 1 April 1910.
11. Ibid.
12. Ibid.

## Chapter 4
## Colliers and Magpies

1.  *Barnsley Chronicle,* 23 April 1910.
2.  Ibid.
3.  Correspondent to *The Times,* 23 April 1910.
4.  Ibid.
5.  *Barnsley Chronicle,* 23 April 1910
6.  Ibid.
7.  Ibid.
8.  Ibid, 30 April 1910.
9.  *The Times,* 25 April 1910.
10. Ibid.
11. *Barnsley Chronicle,* 23 April 1910.
12. Ibid.
13. *The Times,* 25 April 1910. John Thomas (Dickie) Downs made one appearance for England, much later in his career, playing in a 2–0 win over Ireland on 23 October 1920.
14. G. Firth. 1978. *Oakwell. The Official History of Barnsley Football Club.*
15. *Barnsley Chronicle,* 30 April 1910.
16. Ibid.
17. FA Cup Final replays continued into the 1990s before being replaced by a penalty shoot out. Arsenal was the first winner of an FA Cup Final in this manner, defeating Manchester United in 2005, and then Liverpool beat West Ham United in the same manner in 2006.
18. *Daily Mirror,* 29 April 1910.
19. Ibid.
20. B. Butler. 1998. *The Official Illustrated History of the FA Cup.*
21. *Barnsley Chronicle,* 30 April 1910.
22. Ibid.

## Chapter 5
## Replays and replays

1.  W. Shakespeare. *A Midsummer Night's Dream.* Act III, scene 2.

Shakespeare's text differs by one word; I cite the text as it appears in *Lifting the Cup*.
2.   *Swindon Advertiser*, 9 May 1910.
3.   *Borough Press (Swindon)*, 7 May 1910.
4.   *The Auto* quoted in *Swindon Advertiser*, 12 May 1910.
5.   Ibid.
6.   *Daily Express*, 1 April 1912.

## Chapter 6
## The 1912 Cup Final

1.   *The Times*, 22 April 1911.
2.   *Daily Mirror*, 22 April 1912.
3.   *The Times*, 20 April 1912.
4.   Sporting Intelligence, *The Times*, 22 April 1912.
5.   Ibid.
6.   Ibid.
7.   Anne Wade, personal communication.
8.   Scottish Screen Archive, Glasgow.
9.   *Daily Mirror*, 22 April 1912.
10.  Sporting Intelligence, *The Times*, 22 April 1912.
11.  Ibid.
12.  *Daily Mirror*, 22 April 1912.
13.  *The Sporting Chronicle*, 22 April 1912.
14.  Following 1910, 1911 and 1912, the next FA Cup final replay was not until 1970.
15.  *The Sporting Chronicle*, 22 April 1912.
16.  *The Yorkshire Evening News*, 25 April 1912.
17.  *The Sporting Chronicle*, 22 April 1912.
18.  Ibid.
19.  Ibid.
20.  Ibid.
21.  *Green Un' Cup Special*, 17 February 1990.
22.  *The Yorkshire Evening News*, 25 April 1912.

## Chapter 7
## The girl next door

1. *Oxford Dictionary of National Biography*, entry on Colin Campbell McKechnie Veitch (1881–1938), Tony Mason.
2. *Barnsley Chronicle*, 7 May 1910.
3. George Utley made one appearance for England, playing in a 2–1 defeat to Ireland on 15 February 1913. Dickie Downs was selected seven years later.
4. G. Firth. 1978. Oakwell. *The Official History of Barnsley Football Club*.
5. *Barnsley Chronicle*, 2 May 1914.
6. Ibid, 18 April 1914.

## Chapter 8
## Scandal at Liverpool

1. *Liverpool Echo*, 13 May 1914.
2. Ibid.
3. *Liverpool Daily Post and Mercury*, 21 December 1914.
4. *Liverpool Football Echo*, 19 December 1914.
5. Ibid, 19 December 1914.
6. Ibid, 26 December 1914.
7. Ibid.
8. Ibid.
9. Ibid.
10. Law Report of 6 July 1917, *The Times*, 7 July 1917.
11. *Manchester Sporting Chronicle*, 1 April 1915.
12. Quoted in S. Inglis. 1995. *Soccer in the Dock. A History of British Football Scandals* 1900 to 1965.
13. *The Sporting Chronicle*, 3 April 1915.
14. O'Connell was later manager of FC Barcelona during the Spanish Civil War.
15. *Liverpool Daily Post*, 3 April 1915.
16. *The Sporting Chronicle*, 3 April 1915.
17. Law Report of 6 July 1917, in *The Times*, 7 July 1917.

## Chapter 9
## Football and war

1. *Evening News* cited in *The Times*, 3 September 1914.
2. *The Times*, 7 November 1914.
3. *T.P.'s Weekly*, 12 September 1914 cited in C. Veitch. 1985. *Journal of Contemporary History* 20, 363–378.
4. *The Times*, 28 November 1914.
5. *Manchester Evening News*, 7 April 1915.
6. The professional football leagues also continued in Germany. While the debates raged in Britain about continuation of football, *The Times* on 28 November 1914 noted that the *Berlin Lokalanzeiger* had listed the forthcoming league matches and the prospects of the various teams. Several of the most popular players in Germany by then, however, had been drafted into the army, whereas in Britain conscription was not implemented until 1916.
7. C. Veitch. 1985. *Journal of Contemporary History* 20, 363–378.
8. Eric Doig, personal communication.
9. *Liverpool Daily Post,* 3 April 1915.
10. *Liverpool Football Echo,* 3 April 1915.
11. *Liverpool Daily Post,* 12 April 1912.
12. *The Football Post (Nottingham)*, 9 September 1916.
13. From 1918 diary of Company Sergeant Major Frederick W. Wiehl quoted with permission of Kevin Dowson and Maggie Tyler. Copyright Kevin Dowson.
14. *Bedfordshire Times and Independent*, 11 February 1916. Sourced by John Wainwright.
15. Ibid.
16. Quoted in C. Veitch. 1985. *Journal of Contemporary History* 20, 363–378.

## Chapter 10
## The Hindenberg Line

1. Sir Douglas Haig's Final Despatch, 21 March 1919, issued as supplement to *The London Gazette,* 8 April 1919.
2. F. E. Whitton. 1926. *History of the 40th Division.* pp. 88–89.

3.    J. Horsfall and N. Cave. 2002. *Battleground Europe: Bourlon Wood*. p. 15
4.    Ibid. p. 23.
5.    Quoted in F.E. Whitton. 1926. *History of the 40ᵗʰ Division*. p. 111.
6.    H.G. Wells 1933. *The Shape of Things to Come*.

## Chapter 11
## Bourlon Wood

1.    F.E. Whitton. 1926. *History of the 40ᵗʰ Division*. pp. 136–145.
2.    *Worksop Guardian*, 6 December 1918.
3.    War Diary, 40ᵗʰ Divisional Trench Mortar Batteries, National Archives, Kew.
4.    Ibid.
5.    Ibid.
6.    A. Hitler. 1925. *Mein Kampf*.

## Chapter 12
## The Advance to Victory

1.    Herbert Asquith's Guildhall Speech, 9 November 1914. Quoted from *The Times* 14 October 1918.
2.    Quoted in F.E. Whitton. 1926. *History of the 40ᵗʰ Division*. p. 304.
3.    Ibid. p. 304.
4.    War Diary, 40ᵗʰ Divisional Trench Mortar Batteries, National Archives, Kew.
5.    Quoted in F.E. Whitton. 1926. *History of the 40ᵗʰ Division*. p. 307.
6.    F.E. Whitton. 1926. *History of the 40ᵗʰ Division*. pp. 307–308.
7.    Ibid. p. 309.
8.    War Diary, 40ᵗʰ Divisional Trench Mortar Batteries, National Archives, Kew.
9.    Obituaries, *Worksop Guardian*, 6 December 1918.

## Epilogue

1.    *Daily Express*, 13 April 1970.
2.    Obituaries, *Worksop Guardian*, 6 December 1918.